Supporting children with EAL in the early years

by Judith Harries

Contents

Introduction	2
Chapter One: EAL in the early years	4
Chapter Two: Singing songs and rhymes	10
Chapter Three: Listening Skills	22
Chapter Four: Real rhythms	25
Chapter Five: Making music	32
Chapter Six: Exploring colour and patterns	38
Chapter Seven: Using a variety of media and materials	44
Chapter Eight: Construction workers	54
Chapter Nine: Movement and dance	60
Chapter Ten: Drama and expressive play	64
Resources	68

Published by Practical Pre-School Books, A Division of MA Education Ltd, St Jude's Church, Dulwich Road, Herne Hill, London, SE24 0PB.

Tel: 020 7738 5454

www.practicalpreschoolbooks.com

© MA Education Ltd 2018

Design: Mary Holmes **fonthill**creative 01722 717036

All images © MA Education Ltd. with the exception of p10 (bottom picture) © Monkey Business/Adobe Stock; p11 © Gorilla/Adobe Stock; p13 © thingamajiggs/Adobe Stock; p14 © Galina Barskaya/Adobe Stock; p19 © Noam/Adobe Stock; p25 (top picture) © biker3/Adobe Stock; (bottom picture) © Arkady Chubykin/Adobe Stock; p26 © Robert Kneschke/Adobe Stock; p27 © korobula/Adobe Stock; p32 (top picture) © highwaystarz/Adobe Stock; p34 © Don/Adobe Stock; p35 © oksix/Adobe Stock; p37 © Smole/Adobe Stock; p39 © spyrakot/Adobe Stock; p46 © DrUGO_1.0/Adobe Stock; p48 © Drobot Dean/Adobe Stock; p49 © milankubicka/Adobe Stock; p51 © oksix/Adobe Stock; p52 © mashiki/Adobe Stock; p53 © EvgeniiAnd/Adobe Stock; p54 (bottom picture) © Chepko Danil/Adobe Stock; p55 © auremar/Adobe Stock; p56 © bennymarty/Adobe Stock; p57 © Photographee.eu/Adobe Stock; p63 © Tamara Sushko/Adobe Stock; p64 (top picture) © tatsushi/Adobe Stock; p67 © Arto/Adobe Stock.

All rights reserved. No part of this publication may be reproduced, stored in a retrieval system, or transmitted by any means, electronic, mechanical, photocopied or otherwise, without the prior permission of the publisher.

ISBN 978-1-909280-98-4

Introduction

This book presents guidance for EYFS practitioners, both new and more experienced, and aims to help settings create a stimulating learning environment that is welcoming and inclusive for all children. Children with EAL pose an exciting challenge to a setting, especially if there are several children, each with a different language. It is crucial that all children feel their language and culture are respected and valued and some cultural differences are outlined here to assist with this understanding.

The preliminary section includes helpful information on the early stages of learning English as an additional language and suggests many ways to support children with EAL and their families so that they feel accepted, secure and welcome. The role of the key worker is outlined as is the importance of home visits as a way to break down barriers.

The main objective of the book is to provide a unique and varied batch of creative activities for early years practitioners to use that involve ideas and skills from the Early Learning Goal for Expressive Arts and Design. These simple and practical activities are presented in an accessible format that staff can dip into and return to as an ongoing resource throughout the EYFS and continuing into KS1. **Supporting children with EAL in the early years** shows ways to help practitioners create a fully inclusive learning environment, where children with EAL will be able to access and engage in activities that all children enjoy. However, the book is an ideal resource for 'all learners', providing a wealth of opportunities for children to thrive and succeed at every level of communication.

Early stages of learning English

All children with EAL will learn English at their own pace, often dependent initially on how fluent they are in their home language. Many EYFS children are just coping with their first experiences of conversation with new peers and adults using their first language, so it can be particularly

Introduction

bewildering to be faced with the demands of a second language. There is debate as to whether children benefit from being completely immersed into the second language or encouraged to use both. This will depend on the provision at your setting. I feel that they should be encouraged to retain and develop their first language and many basic concepts will already have been learned and processed in the original language that can be applied to learning English.

Many of the activities in this book encourage children to share their home language as they go along. Remember to start with what each child already knows and are interested in, and use that as a way to develop their learning.

The first stage that many children with EAL go through is a 'silent' period, when they will use gestures, signs, and possibly some words in their home language. This is not a passive time as they will be actively listening and watching as they explore this new environment and often will be able to understand more than they can speak. It is important not to pressure them to speak at this time and be patient as it can last for up to six months. They may begin to echo particular words or short phrases such as 'drink' or 'toilet' and then go onto using small chunks or phrases with meaning such as 'My turn', 'Home soon' or 'Mummy come now?' They may start to join in with refrains in stories, songs and rhymes and lots of group singing at this stage can encourage them to 'have a go' without worrying about being heard. Imitation is a key part of learning and they will enjoy copying the other children's words and actions.

Correct intonation and prosody can emerge before meaningful sentences. Basic question words are some of the first to be used along with independent phrases such as 'I like…' or 'I want…'. Encourage 'scaffolding' when the listener sympathetically supplies any missing words or phrases to support emerging conversation.

Chapter One:
EAL in the early years

Positive relationships

Setting and home visits

Most settings will encourage children and their parents to visit on at least one occasion prior to their starting date so that the children are familiar with some adults, the layout of the building and other practicalities. Starting at a new setting is a scary time for both the child and the parents/carers, and not being able to communicate, understand what is being said, or read letters and notices can make it worse. Put up welcome signs in multiple languages, introduce key workers and set out a mix of familiar, favourite, and fun activities for children to explore.

Many settings also offer a 'home visit' and these can be invaluable for establishing a partnership between home and setting. The key worker can meet the child in his or her own environment and find out about toys, interests, pets, and siblings, as well as key pointers about their cultural background. It's a good opportunity to get to know parents and try to help them feel they can approach the key worker with any concerns.

Home visits should always involve two members of staff including one who knows some of the child's home language if possible. Take along photos of the setting to talk about and a puppet or toy to help interaction with the child. Use this opportunity to help parents fill in any paperwork, including medical and dietary requirements and fill in an information sheet with details about the child's name (spelling and pronunciation is really important), their main likes and dislikes, the language the parent uses with the child, and any religious and cultural beliefs. Some families will not want a home visit and this view should of course be respected.

Chapter One: EAL in the early years

The role of the key worker

The key worker has a particularly important role in forging 'positive relationships' when working with EAL children and their families. It starts at the pre-visit or home visit and it is important to quickly establish a friendly and approachable manner with parents/carers and child. Make sure you know how to pronounce the child's name, learn how to greet the family in their home language if you can, and be aware of some of the child's interests. Refer back to facts you learned at the home visit. Support services are available from local authorities to help settings support EAL families such as Ethnic Minority Achievement (EMA) teams.

If the child is starting mid-term, pair them with a child or supportive group that you trust, as they will be a friendly guide or provide role-models. Don't expect or demand speech too early and allow for a period of silent but active listening as they adjust. Use lots of non-verbal cues and have picture fans to hand. Have a digital tablet available so you can check online translations and allow children to hear their home language. Take care not to misinterpret facial expressions or gestures and be sensitive to cultural differences with regard to personal space (see page 6). Spend one to one time helping the child become familiar with routines, such as snack and playtime, where the toilets are situated, hanging up belongings on peg, and so on.

The child with EAL
What a child in your setting may be thinking…

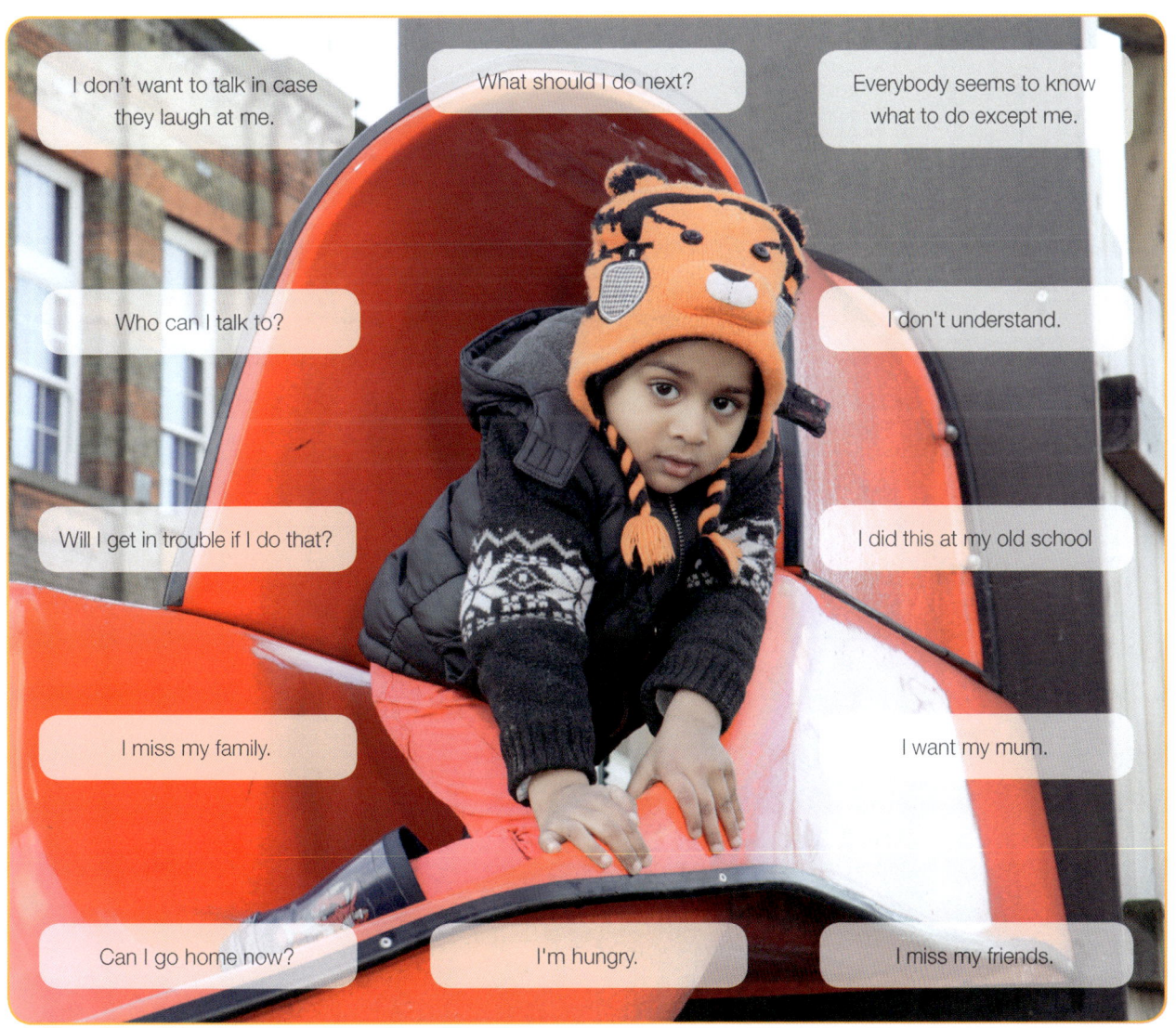

- I don't want to talk in case they laugh at me.
- What should I do next?
- Everybody seems to know what to do except me.
- Who can I talk to?
- I don't understand.
- Will I get in trouble if I do that?
- I did this at my old school
- I miss my family.
- I want my mum.
- Can I go home now?
- I'm hungry.
- I miss my friends.

Chapter One: EAL in the early years

Enabling environments

Creating a suitable environment for learning

Every early years setting seeks to create a stimulating environment for learning that is inclusive and helps children to feel safe, supported and engaged. The first step is to aim for positive relationships between practitioners, children and parents, and between the children themselves.

It is always important to observe children in order to inform planning and provide appropriate activities that foster their interests and develop their learning. Activities should be accessible, challenging and achievable.

Ways to support children with EAL and their families

The key thing to remember is to celebrate the linguistic diversity that children with EAL and their families bring to your setting. Provide a range of opportunities for children to use their home language so that the development of English and other languages support one another.

'Supporting continued development of first language and promoting the use of first language for learning enables children to access learning opportunities within the EYFS and beyond through their full language repertoire.' (Primary National Strategy, 2007)

Aim to provide play and learning resources that reflect children's cultural identity, for instance books, posters, labels and role-play equipment. Provide signs and notices in the home language for children and their families and offer translation services if required.

Ensure there are plenty of opportunities to use an outdoor area as children are often less inhibited when using language in an outdoor environment. Many of the creative activities in this book can be taken outside.

'Practitioner observations have shown that children commonly make at least five times as many utterances outdoors as they do inside.' (Primary National Strategy, 2007)

Remember to use non-verbal cues alongside words when giving instructions. Use hand gestures for 'stand' or 'sit' and 'line up', rubbing tummy seems to be a well accepted signal for feeling hungry and copying facial expressions can also help children express their feelings without words.

Cultural differences

It is important to be aware of some cultural differences which may affect how children react to some facial expressions, gestures, body contact and awareness of personal space. Some of these are summarised below:

- **physical contact** - Some children are uncomfortable with physical contact for cultural reasons. Muslim women and girls do not like to shake hands. In Nepal, the head is thought to be sacred and should not be touched.
- **eye contact** - If a child avoids eye contact it may be to show respect to their teacher rather than a sign that they are not listening. Try not to insist that a child looks directly at you if it clearly makes them uncomfortable.
- **smile** - Some children will smile even when being told off, again to show respect, so try not to misinterpret it as disrespectful.

Chapter One: EAL in the early years

- **nod** - A child may nod their head to acknowledge that you are talking to them but it doesn't mean they understand what you are trying to say.
- **answer** - Some children won't answer unless they are sure they have the 'right' answer to avoid 'losing face'.
- **aggression** - Playtime can be very stressful if a child's English is limited, and if non-verbal means are not working some children may resort to aggressive behaviour in an attempt to make themselves understood.
- **eating** - Some children may only be used to eating with their own family and feel unhappy eating with the other children. Always check out any particular dietary requirements.
- **animals** - Different cultures hold a variety of views about animals, some avoid contact with them, others revere certain animals, so check first.

How Expressive Arts and Design activities help language development in children with EAL

The two Early Learning Goals for Expressive Arts and Design cover a wide range of activities:

> Children sing songs, make music and dance, and experiment with ways of changing them. They safely use and explore a variety of materials, tools and techniques, experimenting with colour, design, texture, form and function.
>
> Children use what they have learnt about media and materials in original ways, thinking about uses and purposes. They represent their own ideas, thoughts and feelings through design and technology, art, music, dance, role play and stories.
>
> (Development Matters in the EYFS, 2012)

This book aims to visit each of these goals and provides activities under the following headings: **Singing songs and rhymes**; **Listening skills**; **Real rhythms**; **Making music**; **Exploring colour and patterns**; **Using a variety of media and materials**; **Construction workers**; **Movement and dance**; **Drama and expressive play**.

There are many reasons why I chose to focus on expressive arts activities when compiling this book, not least being my 25 years experience teaching music and drama to children aged from 9 months to eleven years! I will attempt to set down some other reasons below.

I include a number of '**echoing**' activities. Echoing is a key part of learning any language. Babies learn by echoing their parents, many children with children. In early stages of learning English they go through a silent period. Their brains are busy storing information and it is certainly not a passive stage. After observing and listening they will tentatively start to 'echo' or copy sounds, words and phrases that they hear.

Listening and musical activities are recognised as an important part of learning **phonics** as they increase children's ability to distinguish between sounds including 'phonemes' or the sounds of individual letters. Studies have also found that children involved in 'free-choice' musical play will frequently co-ordinate their play with other children using non-verbal means such as gestures, eye contact, body movement and facial expressions (Susan Young, 2008). This suggests that exploring music together is a great activity for children to communicate non-verbally as they process their language skills and helps to boost self-esteem. I have

Chapter One: EAL in the early years

witnessed a newly-arrived child with EAL who relaxed and joined in with his peers for the very first time when using a drum to express himself rather than words.

Children's creative development will be enriched if they are given the opportunity to '*experiment with a variety of instruments and other sound sources*' as recommended for all four year olds by the NAfME (National Association for Music Education).

Once language begins to emerge, the use of songs is an essential part of learning for children with EAL. There are lots of examples of how to use **songs and rhymes** in your setting: from using well-known songs and rhymes, adding new words to existing tunes and some opportunities to writing your own. Many songs use repeated refrains and these can be a perfect opportunity for EAL children to make their first utterances without fear of being overheard in the crowd!

Songs can also be used to help children identify different **routines** in the day such as taking the register, play time or lining up for assembly. Singing instructions and using repeated vocal patterns or chants help children with EAL to recognise what you want them to do long before they understand the meaning of some of the words. Saying names, colours, numbers and other sequences of words **in rhythm** can help children literally get their tongues around new words. You can even introduce a range of clapped rhythms to indicate certain instructions, for example 'llll l - ' = 'Time to tidy up' or
' l l l l llll l l' = 'Line up, line up, everybody line up'.

Experimenting with colour and design through **visual art** activities is all part of making sense of the world. Young children come to an understanding of their acquired world through hands-on experience, **playing** with the materials and exploring their feelings. Children with EAL can express themselves through artistic activities in a more genuine and free way, without the limitations of emerging language.

How to use this book

Each chapter in the book includes several different activities based on the theme linked to Expressive Arts and Design that can be dipped into as required. Many of them present opportunities for practitioners to sit alongside children as they play, and interact with appropriate dialogue or initiate conversation in a more informal situation. Each activity is presented in the following format:

What you need: includes a full list of materials needed to carry out the various activities. Try and find them all before starting an activity, and make common sense substitutions where required.

What to do: provides 'step by step' instructions on how to carry out the activities with a group of children. There are often several activities included under the banner of one learning objective and they can be worked through or 'cherry picked' as the practitioner chooses.

Whatever next: presents some follow up activities related to the theme that will extend the children's learning further.

All rounders: looks at ways the activities relate to the other areas of the EYFS: Communication and Language (**CL**); Physical Development (**PD**); Personal, Social and Emotional Development (**PSED**); Literacy (**L**); Mathematics (**M**) and Understanding the World (**UW**). It also includes suggestions for new ideas that develop different ELGs.

Chapter One: EAL in the early years

There are also some teaching strategies that are used frequently in the book and I have outlined them here:

Echo clapping: Children learn many things, including language, from copying others. Echo clapping is a strategy I regularly use in my teaching. It is a useful resource for working with children with EAL who may struggle to follow verbal instructions. Attract the children's attention at the start or end of an activity by clapping a short rhythm pattern for them to copy or 'echo'. Different rhythms can be used to signify different events such as 'snack time' or 'sit on the carpet'. Echo clapping is included as an activity on page 26.

Puppets: are a great way to bring less confident children 'out of their shells'. They may feel easier saying first words or expressing feelings to a puppet rather than another child or adult. Sometimes if the group focus is on a puppet, it takes the attention away from them and can help a more anxious child to relax. However, If the thought of using a puppet makes you feel anxious, try practising at home first in front of a mirror! You will soon gain in confidence. Many singing and speaking activities benefit from the use of a special puppet, known to the children, that can model responses (see 'Puppet Power', on page 67).

Talk partners: is a strategy used in most settings now and is a key part of helping all children to feel more involved in their learning. Start the week by picking new talk partners and get children to sit on the carpet next to their talk partner. Display the partners on a board so children can check who they are working with later.

Pupil talk is central to active learning. Establishing talk partners is often the first step teachers take in experimenting with formative assessment, as it is relatively straightforward to embark on and the impact can be seen immediately. (Shirley Clarke, 2008)

Choosing Hat: is a great way of choosing children for activities without the fear of missing anyone out or showing favour. It randomises selection and helps all children feel included. Write the name of each child onto a lollipop stick or card and place them in the hat. When you need to select a child for an activity, just pick a card or let the children help you.

Chapter Two: Singing songs and rhymes

Singing songs and rhymes together is a key activity in the daily routine of most early years settings. It is a time to bond socially, to share special events such as birthdays and other celebrations, and can be used to reinforce learning in many areas of the curriculum. Use songs to sing about names, feelings, days of the week, the weather, phonics, numbers, parts of the body and the natural world, and try to add actions as often as possible. Allow children space and opportunities to sing and vocalise on their own as they play.

How to help children with EAL: Singing in a group, and joining in fun actions, is an ideal informal context for children with EAL to begin to communicate as they settle into your setting.

You can:
- make up your own songs using new words to existing tunes
- find repeated song refrains that encourage all children to join in
- use simple songs or chants to identify routines during the school day.

Supporting children with EAL in the early years

Chapter Two: **Singing songs and rhymes**

Snap your fingers

Share a well-known finger rhyme and encourage social interaction. Invite children to work with a partner and practise saying the rhyme together.

What you need:

- A familiar finger rhyme
- Two bird finger puppets
- Small strips of paper
- Felt pens
- Glue or sticky tape
- Drum

What to do:

1. This activity works with a small group or the whole group sat together in a circle.
2. Start with a well-known finger rhyme such as *Two little dicky birds sitting on a wall, One named Peter, one named Paul. Fly away Peter, fly away Paul. Come back Peter, come back Paul.*
3. Demonstrate the rhyme using two bird finger puppets. Ask the children to snap their fingers to scare away the birds. If they struggle to snap their fingers suggest an alternative sound such as tongue click or two fingers tapped on palm of the hand.
4. Show the children how to use their two index fingers as the birds, make them fly away behind their backs one by one, and then return.
5. Encourage lots of repetition. Don't worry if children with EAL just join in with the actions. Invite children to work with a partner or friend and show each other the rhyme.
6. Provide children with small strips of paper to make their own finger puppet birds. Ask them to draw bird faces with funny eyes and a beak.
7. Join the strips into finger rings for the children to use as finger puppets when they say the rhyme. Alternatively, let the children use the bird finger puppets.
8. Add a drum beat to the rhyme and let children take turns to snap their fingers in time to the drum, while a volunteer is saying the rhyme as a solo.

Whatever next

- Ask the children to think of a different animal and change a few of the words in the rhyme, for instance: *Two little butterflies sitting on a plant, one named Greta, one named Grant, Fly away…*
- Keep to the same structure but change the actions too! *Two little lions hiding in a den, One named Leo and one named Len. Out jumped Leo, out jumped Len, In went Leo, in went Len.* Have fun acting out the rhymes.
- Invite children to share any other finger rhymes that they know from home or nursery. Try 'Tommy Thumb', 'Peter hammers with one hammer', 'I have ten little fingers', and 'Little Johnny dances'.

All rounders

CL: Point out the rhyming words in the rhyme. Can the children think of a word that rhymes with their name? Take care to use correct pronunciation of children's names. Don't discount nonsense words at this stage.

M: This is a good activity for reinforcing the concept of number one and two. Say the rhyme and stop to emphasise the numbers 1 and 2 as you go.

UW: Look at images of birds from around the world online, particularly from children's home countries. Encourage children with EAL to use their first language to tell you the names of birds.

Chapter Two: Singing songs and rhymes

Echo singing

Invite the children to copy or echo each time you sing. Start with a simple greeting song and encourage children with EAL to echo their talk partners.

What you need:

- Confidence to sing out loud
- Talk partner board
- Puppet

What to do:

1. Try these words to the tune of 'Rain, rain, go away':
   Hello everyone, [hello everyone],
   Welcome to Monday, [welcome to Monday]
   Change the day of the week accordingly. Challenge the children to tell you the day!
2. Model singing the echo song with a puppet singing the echoes. Add humour by making him go wrong a few times, such as interrupting, or singing the wrong thing. Then model the puppet echo singing perfectly!
3. Invite children to sit next to their talk partners. Refer to the talk partner board to remind them of this week's partnerships.
4. Ask them to sing the greeting song with their talk partners. Can they replace 'everyone' with the name of their partner? Help children with EAL to practise saying and singing each other's names.
5. Use this song to take the register to the tune of 'I hear thunder'.
   Hello (child's name)? [echo]
   How are you? [echo]
   Hope you're feeling fine? [echo]
   And you too! [echo]
6. Start by singing the song with all the children singing the echoes together. When they are more confident invite children to sing the last line on their own.
7. Invite some children with EAL to share how to say hello or an equivalent greeting in their language and change the beginning of the song. Go to www.pocketcultures.com for help on saying hello in different languages.

Whatever next

- Sing some other well-known echo songs such as 'Frère Jacques', 'I hear thunder', 'Charlie over the ocean' or make up your own.
- Invite confident children to be the leader and try some echo singing. The others have to copy everything the leader says or sings. Add actions.
- Talk about the science of echoes. Play children a video from YouTube of a sound echoing in a tunnel. Sound bounces off the walls and comes back to your ears. Ask the children to stand in a line or a circle and send an echo around. Can they make the word or phrase get steadily quieter as it passes like an echo?

All rounders

PSED: This is a good way for children to learn each other's names at the beginning of the year or term. Make sure you know how to pronounce the children's names and which familiar name they are using.
CL: Read *Little Beaver and the Echo* by Amy MacDonald. Act out the story and let children take turns to make the echo sounds.
M: The greeting song will help children to learn the names of days of the week and begin to understand the concept of time. Encourage EAL children to share the names of the days of the week in their language with the group.

Chapter Two: Singing songs and rhymes

Two-tone tunes

Use the two notes of the 'cuckoo' call to help children echo using their voices and other musical instruments.

What you need:

- Two notes to sing or play
- A selection of tuned musical instruments: xylophones, chime bars or hand chimes, boomwhackers, etc.

What to do:

1. Work with a small group of children with EAL or the whole class seated in a circle.
2. Explain that you are going to try some echo singing and playing. Invite children to copy what you sing or play. Refer back to the echo songs in 'Echo singing', page 12.
3. Start by singing two notes: (G - E) a falling interval most recognisable as the early cuckoo call. Use the words 'soh' and 'me' instead of the note names and try the sol-fa hand signs. The higher note 'soh' - palm of hand, held horizontally, facing you in front of the face, and the lower note 'me' - palm of hand, held horizontally, palm down in front of the chest.
4. Invite children with EAL to copy you as you sing and sign. Try lots of repetitions until they gain in confidence. Emphasise that the 'soh' note and hand sign are higher than the 'me' note.
5. Challenge children to be the leader and use their voice and hands to lead the singing.
6. Introduce some tuned instruments that play the same notes - 'soh' and 'me' (G - E). Chime bars, hand chimes, xylophones, keyboard, boomwhackers will all use these notes.
7. Play a pattern using the two tones and invite children to echo using 'soh' and 'me'. Here are some to start you off:
   soh me soh me...me me soh...me soh me -
8. Let the children take turns to play patterns using the instruments for the other children to echo.
9. If you have two sets of instruments, show children how to copy the two-tone patterns played on the chime bars on a different instrument instead of using their voices.
10. Repeat the game with two new notes, high C and low C. Emphasise the contrast in pitch by asking children to stand up and sit down in response.

Whatever next

- Set up an echo play corner in your setting. Invite children to visit as part of their free play and work with a friend or talk partner creating echo patterns. Put sets of instruments in the corner for the children to use. Can they record their echoes on a tablet?
- Let children write out some simple patterns using 'soh' and 'me' cards for each other to play.
- Try some simple science by showing children that the difference between the two tones or notes is the size of the instrument. The shorter or smaller bars play high sounds. The longer or bigger bars play low sounds. This is a basic principle of pitch that most young children can grasp.

All rounders

PSED: Use this activity to practise taking turns. Try to ensure that everybody gets a turn by using a register to check or pull names out of the 'choosing hat'.
L: Children can practise writing skills writing echo patterns for each other to play. Can they think of other symbols to use rather than 'soh' and 'me' related to high and low?
M: Try some measuring activities to compare the sizes of different instruments such as hand chimes and boomwhackers.

Chapter Two: Singing songs and rhymes

Sing it, do it

Use songs to give instructions or mark routines in the nursery day. All children will become familiar with the songs as they settle into the setting.

What you need:

- Some suitable songs sung to well-known tunes
- Puppet

What to do:

1. These are activities for all the group to listen to, join in and follow instructions.
2. Every nursery setting has routines that can be signalled with a song. Start with greetings or the register (see Echo Singing, page 12). Use the puppet to sing them if you prefer.
3. Try some of these songs:
4. Snack time (Tune: 'The Flintstones')
   Snack time, now it's snack time.
   Come and sit and share your snack with me.
   Snack time, now it's snack time.
   Share a snack with our family.
   This also works for lunch time.
   Lunch time, now it's lunch time.
   Come and join us for some tasty food.
   Lunch time, now it's lunch time.
   Eating this will put you in a good mood.
5. Time to tidy up (Tune: 'A hunting we will go')
   It's time to tidy up, X2
   It's time to tidy up now,
   It's time to tidy up.
   Try these alternative 3rd lines:
   Make the table tidy oh/Tidy up the bricks please/Help each other tidy up
6. Lining up (Tune: 'It's raining')
   Line up, line up,
   Everybody line up.
   Time for us to get in line
   And go to assembly/go outside for playtime/go to the hall for PE
7. Joining the circle (Tune: 'She'll be coming round the mountain')
   We are joining the circle, yes we are, [yes we are] X2
   We are joining the circle, joining the circle,
   Joining the circle, yes we are [yes we are].
   This is a good song for making a circle for group circle time. Change action to 'sitting on the carpet' or 'getting changed for PE' to suit the moment.

Whatever next

- Involve children with EAL in making up new songs with you for different routines and activities in your setting.
- Encourage children to write their own songs about any topic. Show them how to film each other singing using a tablet.
- Sing the tunes to 'dum, dum' or 'la' without the words. Can the children still recognise which 'command' you are giving?

All rounders

PSED: Try different ways to line up such as 'in register order' or alternating 'boy, girl, boy, girl' and so on. Invite children to think of other new ways to line up.
CL: Introduce words about the time of day - morning, afternoon, evening, night, dawn, dusk, and help children with EAL to understand where they fit.
M: Use these songs and routines as an opportunity to talk about time with all the children. Point out the time on the clock at play time, lunch time and home time so the children get more familiar with them.

Chapter Two: Singing songs and rhymes

Heads, shoulders, knees and toes

Use this well known action song to help children with EAL learn about the different parts of the body and have fun mixing and matching the words and actions.

What you need:

- Song words or version of the song online at www.bbc.co.uk/learning/schoolradio/subjects/earlylearning/nurserysongs
- Cardboard
- Felt pens
- Pictures of parts of the body
- Scissors, glue

What to do:

1. Sit all the children in a circle or on the carpet.
2. Teach the song by singing each line for children to repeat or watch a version online.
   Heads, shoulders, knees and toes, [knees and toes], X2
   And eyes, and ears, and mouth and nose,
   Heads, shoulders, knees and toes, [knees and toes].
3. Add the actions by pointing at each part of the body as it is mentioned. There are only eight words to remember. Try not to over correct children's pronunciation as this can discourage children with EAL from singing.
4. When the children are more familiar with the song and actions try missing one of the words, for instance 'head', and just point at the relevant body part.
5. Repeat and miss out two words, 'heads, shoulders', and so on.
6. Let children with EAL share the names of the parts of the body and try a version in their home language.
7. Make word and picture flash cards with the children of the different parts of the body to aid learning. Children can take it in turns to hold these up at the appropriate parts of the song.
8. Draw round the outline of one of the children on a large piece of paper. Use paint and collage to create the clothes and features of the child. Add the word and picture cards as labels for the different parts of the body and display on the wall. Add bilingual cards using words from another language.
9. Take photographs of each child on a tablet and let them use the PicCollage app to annotate their portrait with body part labels.

Whatever next

- Try some other songs about the body such as 'One finger, one thumb keep moving', 'Ten little fingers', 'Peter hammers with one hammer', and 'Little Johnny dances'.
- Make some skeleton pictures using white art straws stuck onto black sugar paper. Look at images of skeletons online. Or bring in a real one to look at. Cut different lengths of straws to create a 'stick man'. Add labels for head, shoulders, knees, toes and more.
- Try a skeleton dance using some live music played on wooden instruments or use a recording of 'In the Hall of the Mountain King' by Grieg. Watch the The Skeleton Dance from Walt Disney 'Silly Symphonies' on YouTube for inspiration.

All rounders

PSED: Talk about the words for different types of clothing - and add these labels to the body poster.
CL: Read *Funny Bones* by Allan Ahlberg for more stories and pictures of skeletons. Try watching episodes from the children's TV series.
PD: Help children to put on their coats and fasten them independently. Hold a coat race. Divide children into teams of five or six children. Challenge them all to put on their coats and fasten them before they can go outside. Encourage children to help each other complete the task.

Chapter Two: Singing songs and rhymes

Old MacDonald had a farm

Sing this traditional song about animals and encourage children with EAL to use their voices to make realistic animal sounds.

What you need:

- Song words or version of the song online at www.bbc.co.uk/learning/schoolradio/subjects/earlylearning/nurserysongs
- Plastic or soft toy farm animals
- Cardboard
- Felt pens
- Pictures of animals
- Scissors, glue

What to do:

1. Sit all the children in a circle or on the carpet.
2. Teach the song by singing each line for children to repeat or watch a version online.
   *Old MacDonald had a farm, E I E I O,
   And on that farm he had some cows, E I E I O,
   With a 'moo moo' here and a 'moo moo' there,
   Here a 'moo', there a 'moo', everywhere a 'moo moo',
   Old MacDonald had a farm, E I E I O.*
3. Use the Choosing Hat to select a child to change the animal. What sound will their choice of animal make?
4. Encourage children with EAL to share the sounds of the different animals as they would say in their home language. Is it always the same sound?
5. Make word and picture flash cards with the children showing different animals. Include the name of the animal and its sound in a speech bubble.
6. Ask children to use the flash cards to show which animal is next in the song.
7. Alternatively, they can use plastic or soft toy animals and hold them up in the air when it is their turn to choose an animal.
8. Ask the children to act out the animals with sounds, actions and movements to add to the song.

Whatever next

- Try singing an accumulative version so, as each new animal is added, the song gets longer and the children have to remember the order of the animals.
- Choose a different name, place and type of animal to sing about, for instance: Mrs Wilson had a zoo, E I E I O, And in that zoo she had some penguins, E I E I O, With a 'flap flap' here…
- Use children's names in the farm or zoo and let them choose their own livestock: Nadia Akram had a safari park, E I E I O, And in that park she had some lions, E I E I O…

All rounders

CL: Play a listening game using animal sound effects. Go to www.freesoundeffects.com and click on some different animal sounds for the children to identify. Let them work with a talk partner and see if they both agree on which animal it is.

UW: Let children choose a favourite animal to find out about and create a simple fact file with a picture and some information to share with the other children. Provide some animal books and helpful websites for them to use. Combine the pages into an Animal book.

Chapter Two: Singing songs and rhymes

Five currant buns

Practise counting numbers and explore different types of food with this popular counting and shopping rhyme.

What you need:

- Song words or version of the song online at www.bbc.co.uk/learning/schoolradio/subjects/earlylearning/nurserysongs
- Real or pretend currant buns
- Other real or pretend food to use in rhymes
- Some real or toy money
- A variety of hats

What to do:

1. Sit all the children in a circle or on the carpet.
2. Teach the song by singing each line for children to repeat or watch a version online.
   Five currant buns in the baker's shop,
   Round and fat with a cherry on top.
   Along came _____ with a penny one day.
   Bought a currant bun and took it away.
3. Place a line of five or more currant buns in the middle of the circle or front of class. Invite children with EAL to take turns to come out and buy a bun from the shop.
4. Use the song as a simple structure to buy other types of food in different shops. Let children with EAL suggest a shop and a type of familiar food.
5. Change the wares - Five hot cross buns (Easter time); Five mince pies (Christmas); Five chocolate cookies.
6. Change the shop - Five fat carrots on the market stall, Long and orange, and that's not all… or Five juicy apples in the grocer's shop, round and red and good enough to swap…
7. Encourage children with EAL to share how to count 1 to 5 in their home language. Make some bilingual signs showing number words in different languages. Can children see or hear similarities?
8. Try singing one of the rhymes using numbers in another language.

Whatever next

- Make some sets of paper buns so children can take them home and play the game with their families.
- Try some other number rhymes such as 'Five/Ten fat sausages', 'Five fat peas', '1, 2, 345', 'One man went to mow', 'This old man', and 'One potato, two potato'.
- Learn some nursery rhymes about food and drink such as 'Do you know the muffin man?', 'Polly put the kettle on' and 'I'm a little teapot'.
- Add a bit of drama to the activity by allowing children to choose a hat to wear and a character to play as they go to the shop to buy some food.

All rounders

CL: Set up a baker's shop in the role-play area. Make lots of different salt dough cakes and biscuits to sell. Use folded cake boxes, tins and paper bags. Dress up in aprons and chefs hats. Encourage children to make up conversations between the staff and customers.

PD: Talk about eating healthy food. Make some simple lunch boxes out of sugar paper. Provide children with lots of supermarket magazines to cut up and stick healthy food into their lunch box.

M: One penny is very little to pay for a bun. Talk about different coins and the value of money. Can the children think of a different amount to charge and fit it into the song?

Chapter Two: Singing songs and rhymes

Now I know my ABC

Use this song to help children with EAL to learn the alphabet and play some phonics games.

What you need:

- Song words or version of song sung by a variety of celebrities on Sesame Street.
- Alphabet wall chart or frieze
- White boards and pens
- Puppet

What to do:

1. Sit all the children in a circle or on the carpet.
2. Teach the song by singing each line for children to repeat or watch a version online.
   A B C D E F G,
   H I J K LMNOP ,
   Q R S, T U V,
    W X, Y and Z.
   Now I know my ABC,
   Next time you can sing along with me.
3. Try some singing games using initial letters. Sing this song to the tune of 'Knees Up, Mother Brown' and get children to line up in alphabetical order using their first names. Invite children with EAL to help others pronounce their names.
   My name starts with A (repeat)
   Which letter does your name start with?
   My name starts with A.
4. Invite more confident children to take turns to sing the verse and find all the people who's name starts with the same initial letter as them.
5. Try some drama activities. Introduce the Puppet and choose an adjective with the same initial letter to describe him/her, for instance, Polite Paulina or Happy Hadi. Make the puppet act the part.
6. Invite children to sit with a talk partner. Ask them to take turns to use their fingers to trace different letters on each other's hands. Can they guess them just through touch?
7. Can they think of some alliterative adjectives to describe each other. Ask them to write them down on the white board if they can.
8. Challenge children to stand up and dramatically introduce their partner to the group using the alliterative word and their name. Take turns to act out their new dramatic names?

Whatever next

- Show the children some examples of illustrated letters. Print off some illustrated letters from the internet for them to colour in.
- Invite children with EAL to paint their own artistic initial letters. Provide children with large templates of their initials and show them how to draw round them and then paint using lots of different colours. Extend this activity into paintings or collages of their names.
- Do any of the children recognise the tune of the ABCD song? ('Twinkle, twinkle, little star') Sing the original words. Play the children 'Variations on "Ah, vous dirai-je, Maman" by Mozart. Can they hear the tune again?
- Read *If Rocks could Sing: A Discovered Alphabet* by Lesley McGuirk.

All rounders

CL: Try some phonics games using initial letters such as 'My Grandmother went to the market' and take turns to work through the alphabet listing items she might buy. Change it to 'At the supermarket, ____ bought ____' and use children's names instead. Can they recall the complete shopping list?
PD: Organise an 'Alphabet Hunt' around the setting, inside and outside. Look for everything beginning with certain letters. Take photos of different things you find.
L: Combine photos and drawings into an Alphabet book for your setting. Encourage children to write letters and labels in the book.

Chapter Two: Singing songs and rhymes

I hear thunder

This simple echo song is a great introduction to the English obsession with the weather! Children with EAL will soon catch on to this idea.

What you need:

- Song words or version of the song online at www.bbc.co.uk/learning/schoolradio/subjects/earlylearning/nurserysongs
- Cardboard
- Felt pens

What to do:

1. Sit all the children in a circle or on the carpet.
2. Teach the song by singing each line for children to repeat or watch a version online.
   I hear thunder, I hear thunder,
   Hark don't you, hark don't you?
   Pitter patter raindrops, pitter patter raindrops,
   I'm wet through, so are you.
3. Invite a confident child to be the leader and the rest of the group can echo them.
4. Do the children notice anything different about the last line? It isn't a straight echo because the words change.
5. Ask the children to draw some images of thunder and rain on some flash cards to use with the song. What other stormy weather pictures could they use? How will they draw clouds or lightning?
6. Share the second verse when the weather improves:
   I see blue skies, I see blue skies,
   Way up high, way up high,
   Hurry up the sunshine, hurry up the sunshine,
   We'll soon dry, we'll soon dry.
7. Challenge children to make up a new verse about a different type of weather such as wind, snow or hail.

Whatever next

- Play 'The weather game'. Make up some different actions for different types of weather, for instance: rain - wiggle fingers from high to low; sun - wipe the sweat off brow; thunder - clap hands; wind - pretend to be blown about; cold - shiver and rub arms, and so on.
- Stand in a circle and chant the question 'What is the weather like today?' Children choose a weather action to make. Anybody who has chosen the same weather as the leader has to sit down. Continue the game until there is a winner!
- Invite children with EAL to talk about the weather in their home country. Is it very different from the UK?

All rounders

CL: Watch a weather forecast on TV or online. Show the children a large map of the United Kingdom or a home country for one or more of the children with EAL. Make some weather symbols and let children stick them on the map and then talk about the weather today and tomorrow.

PD: Go outside on a sunny day and look at shadows. Draw round children's shadows with chalk. Play 'Shadow Catchers'. Let children try to jump on each other's shadows. How many can they catch?

UW: Make a weather chart and use the Choosing Hat to select a child each day to draw a picture of the weather. Set up a rain gauge outside to measure the rainfall.

Chapter Two: Singing songs and rhymes

If you're happy and you know it…

This song combines words and actions and is a good one to encourage children with EAL to talk about their feelings and emotions.

What you need:

- Song words or version of the song online at www.bbc.co.uk/learning/schoolradio/subjects/earlylearning/nurserysongs
- Homemade emojis
- Paper plates
- Felt pens
- Puppet
- Sharing Bear

What to do:

1. Sit all the children in a circle or on the carpet.
2. Teach the song by singing each line for children to repeat or watch a version online.
   If you're happy and you know it, clap your hands [repeat]
   If you're happy and you know it,
   And you really want to show it,
   If you're happy and you know it, clap your hands.
3. Try some more verses by adding different actions to each verse: *stamp your feet, nod your head.*
4. For the final verse, sing Do all three, and perform all three of the actions in sequence!
5. Talk about feelings with the children. At circle time, ask children to share things that make them feel happy or sad. Pass a 'Sharing Bear' around the circle and explain that children can only talk when they are holding the toy. If children with EAL don't want to speak they can pass the bear to the next child. Invite the Puppet to join in and share his/her feelings.
6. Look at examples of emojis online. Invite the children to make some emojis using paper plates and felt pens. Can they talk about how their emoji feels.
7. Change the words of the song to a different emotion such as 'sad', 'angry', 'excited', 'scared', and so on. How will the action change to match the feeling?
8. Ask the children in the circle to hold up the appropriate emojis as they sing each version of the song.

Whatever next

- Ask the children how many claps or stamps they do at the end of each line? Change the rhythm and ask children to clap three times to match the word 'happiness' or four times for 'jolly funny'.
- Invite children to make up their own patterns in between the verses using different body percussion - clap, tap, stamp, click, etc.
- Try this new song to the tune of 'Row, row, row the boat'
   Smile, smile, smile with me,
   When you're feeling happy.
   Smile, smile, smile, smile,
   And make your fingers snappy!

   Cry, cry, cry with me
   When you're feeling sad.
   Cry, cry, cry, cry,
   Sorry you feel bad!
   Scowl, scowl, scowl, with me
   When you're feeling cross.
   Scowl, scowl, scowl, scowl,
   You look just like the boss.

All rounders

PSED: Encourage children to be sensitive to each other's feelings as they share stories and experiences. Allow children with EAL to use the paper plate emojis to share how they are feeling.
CL: Use the Sharing Bear at circle time to share other stories and experiences. Encourage children who are nervous about sharing with the whole group to talk to the Bear.

Chapter Two: Singing songs and rhymes

Karaoke corner

Create a performing space in your setting for children to spontaneously sing, chant, recite and perform songs and rhymes to each other.

What you need:

- Space with special performance mat or stage block
- Audience space with bean bag chairs and/or cushions
- Karaoke machine/tablet/CD player
- Pretend microphone (or real if available)
- Song sheets/cards
- Laminator
- Blank cards, pencils, felt pens

What to do:

1. Ask all the children to come and sit together in a circle or on the carpet.
2. Talk about favourite songs and rhymes. Make an annotated list or poster showing their most popular songs. Invite children with EAL to share some traditional songs in their home language.
3. Show them some laminated song cards with prompts on to remind them. Invite children to make some of their own. What will they choose to draw or write on the card for each song?
4. Explain that you are going to set up a Karaoke corner. Ask if any of the children know what 'karaoke' means? Demonstrate it yourself, if you're brave enough!
5. Show the children how to use the equipment in the Karaoke corner in small groups. You can use a karaoke machine, or a microphone, stand, and tablet to film the performances.
6. Encourage children to be spontaneous and spend time singing songs and rhymes they know as well as making up new ones.
7. Talk about different styles of songs such as lullabies, marching songs, action songs, worship songs, popular songs, traditional songs, and so on.
8. Provide dressing up clothes so children can dress up for their performances.
9. Set up a stage area with a raised stage block or special mat for children to stand on when they sing. Add an audience area for children to sit in to watch each other perform.

Whatever next

- Go to www.karafun.co.uk for some ideas for karaoke songs for children.
- Appoint an official photographer from amongst the children to take pictures of the others enjoying the karaoke corner. Include some pictures on the school website so parents can see the children enjoying singing. Make sure you have permission before publishing any photos of the children online.
- Record or film yourself or groups of children singing songs together on the carpet and make these films available in the karaoke corner for others to sing along with. Children will especially enjoy singing along with their friends in this way.

All rounders

PSED: Invite older children higher up the school to come and use the karaoke corner and show off their singing to the children.

M: Do a tally count to record the top ten favourite songs in your setting and display the information as a bar or pie chart. Talk about the names for different groups of singers and introduce the terms solo, duet, trio and quartet.

CL: Encourage children to write reviews of each other's performances. Provide some cards with suggested comments on. Make sure all criticism is constructive!

Chapter Three:
Listening Skills

Children with EAL spend a lot of time listening to the language being spoken around them before they begin to try new sounds and words. Actively listening and then copying sounds is an important part of learning a language. These activities will encourage active listening to sounds, songs, films, stories and rhymes.

How to help children with EAL: Actively encourage children with EAL to share music, songs, stories and rhymes from home and to use their home language alongside English.

You can:
- provide a rich variety of listening material and resources
- encourage children to bring in music from home to share
- allow children time to experiment with different sounds on instruments.

Chapter Three: Listening skills

Listening corner

Set up a comfy corner in your setting for children to visit and listen to stories, songs, and music.

What you need:

- Comfy chairs and cushions
- Curtains and drapes
- Blankets
- Listening equipment: tablets, CD players, computer
- Headphones
- Display board
- Post-it notes
- Pencils

What to do:

1. Choose a quiet space in the setting for your listening corner.
2. Hang curtains and drapes to create a cosy atmosphere so children can relax in comfort and concentrate on listening skills.
3. Provide cushions, pillows, blankets and soft chairs. Encourage the children to make suggestions for how to improve the Listening corner.
4. Set up listening equipment including CD players, computer, tablets and of course, headphones.
5. Take small groups into the area and show children how to use all the equipment.
6. Set them some simple listening challenges to share with the group such as 'Find your favourite song', 'Choose a traditional tale to retell', or 'Share a special song with everybody'.
7. Invite children with EAL to bring in CDs from home with stories and songs in their home language to listen to in the corner.
8. Visit these websites for more resources: www.mamalisa.com or www.learnenglishkids.britishcouncil.org
9. Set up links to short films or YouTube clips of stories and songs in a variety of home languages and English.
10. Encourage children to access the listening corner as part of free play in your setting.
11. Set up a display board on the wall so children can leave post-it notes to each other saying what they have enjoyed listening to and encouraging others to listen.
12. Encourage children to make up their own stories, songs and rhymes and record them for others to listen to in the Listening corner. Let children with EAL use their home language to share with others.

Whatever next

- Provide some listening activities in the listening area such as 'Sound lotto' using a commercial product or your own recorded sounds and pictures to match them. Encourage children with EAL to work with a partner, or in small groups with an adult, and listen to the sounds and identify the pictures.
- Make a matching pairs game using sounds. Fill small plastic containers such as film canisters or small crisp pots with a variety of matching sounds - sand, small bells, gravel, dry rice, coins, peas or beans. Can the children sort the containers into matching pairs just by listening?

All rounders

L: Provide CDs that focus on learning phonics and letter sounds. Try some listening games to develop phonics skills.

M: Provide access to lots of counting songs and rhymes (see Five Currant Buns, on page 17) plus props, so children can use them as they listen.

UW: Allow children to record some songs and stories in their home language for others to listen to. Set up a globe or world map so they can show each other where their home country is situated.

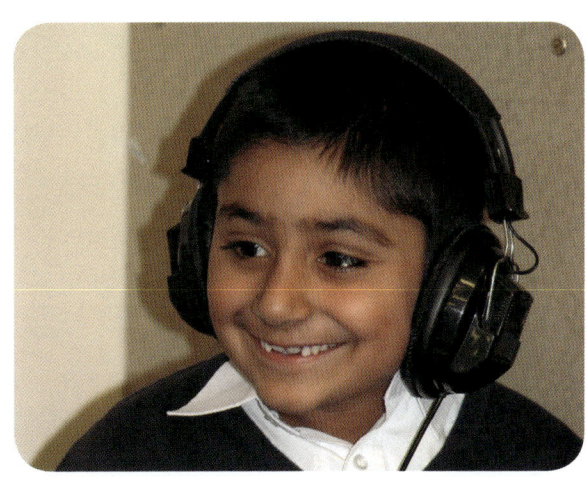

Chapter Three: Listening skills

Sounds of home

This will turn the Listening corner into a place full of sounds: songs, music and instruments from around the world and in particular places represented by children with EAL in your setting.

What you need:

- Access to the Listening corner
- CD player, computer, tablet, etc.
- CDs of music from all over the world
- Headphones
- Musical instruments from around the world
- Camera or tablet

What to do:

1. Explain to the children that the Listening corner is now open to music from all around the world.
2. Invite children with EAL and their families to bring in recordings of traditional music from home. Ask if any members of their family play an instrument and would be happy to come in and show the children.
3. Go online and find some examples of traditional or world music from relevant countries for children to enjoy. Try YouTube, www.worldmusic.net and www.womad.co.uk as resources for listening to world music.
4. Listen to samba music from Brazil, Steel pan music from the Caribbean, Balkan Gypsy music, Bollywood songs and Japanese Taiko drumming. Talk about which music would be good to dance to and try some dance moves, see 'Dance to your daddy', on page 62.
5. Encourage English speaking children to bring in favourite music too and challenge them to find instrumental music as well as songs.
6. Provide children with a selection of world instruments to experiment with, such as djembes, guiros, maracas, castanets, xylophones, cabasas, kalimbas (thumb pianos), ukuleles, rattles, panpipes.
7. Remind children to always handle instruments with care and respect. Encourage the children to self-initiate musical play, either on their own or as a small group.
8. Allow time and opportunity for them to handle the instruments and explore the sounds they can make on their own and together.
9. Film or record the children using the instruments and making music together in small groups.

Whatever next

- Include a set of rainbow bells or chime bars and some tunes with the music written out using colours. Or set up a pentatonic (five note) scale on a xylophone and label the bars C D E G A and write the tunes using these letter names. Simple tunes such as 'Row, row, row the boat' and 'Twinkle, twinkle little star' work really well.
- Let children make some coloured flags from the different countries represented in your setting and add them to a world map on the wall.

All rounders

PD: Share some food from different countries to go with the music. Try different breads from around the world such as Naan from India, Ciabatta from Italy, Banana bread from the Caribbean, Baguette from France, Soda bread from Ireland, Lavash from the Middle East, Pitta bread from the eastern Mediterranean, Rye bread from Germany, and many more.

UW: Provide a world map and put pins in marking where the different musical instruments and types of music come from.

Chapter Four:
Real rhythms

Echo clapping rhythm patterns is a good way to attract the children's attention and to start any activity together. All of the children will soon recognise a rhythm that means 'stop now and listen!' Word rhythms are easy to generate and using children's names helps everybody to feel involved. As children become familiar with the rhythm of a language it eases them into speaking it more fluently.

How to help children with EAL: Rhythm activities will help children with EAL feel included and involved with a sense of immediacy.

You can:
- include children's names in rhythm games
- use rhythm chants to give instructions such as 'sit down on the carpet' or 'line up time.'
- play rhythms together using body percussion, claves and drums.

Supporting children with EAL in the early years

Chapter Four: Real rhythms

Echo clapping

These simple 'copy cat' rhythm activities are a great way for all children, especially children with EAL, to feel involved in making music together.

What you need:

- Space and time for echo clapping
- Simple rhythms to clap
- Choosing Hat
- Enough pairs of pencils for each child

What to do:

1. Ask all the children to sit on the carpet or in a circle so they can see and hear you and each other.
2. Explain that you are going to clap a pattern for them to 'copy cat'. Try clapping four times.
3. Stop and open your hands, palms facing up. This gesture shows the children when to copy.
4. Repeat until everybody has got the idea.
5. Try some more complicated patterns for children to copy. Use your own word phrases to help distinguish between rhythms that you clap such as 'I like fish and chips', 'I like toffee apples', 'Sausages are tasty' or 'Banana ice cream'. Ask children with EAL to share a phrase in their home language to clap.
6. Invite children to have a go at leading the echo clapping. Use the Choosing Hat to select children and make sure everybody has a turn if they want.
7. Try some quieter echo tapping using two fingers on the palm of the hand. Remind children to listen very carefully as the rhythms are quieter.
8. Mix and match claps and taps to vary the volume. Let children lead some mix and match patterns.
9. Ask children to work with a partner and practise copying each other clapping and tapping rhythms. Let them take turns to demonstrate their echo clapping to the rest of the group.

Whatever next

- Play 'Don't clap/tap that one back'. Clap the rhythm 'Don't, clap, that one back!'. Add the words and explain that once the children are familiar with the rhythm the game will begin. The idea is that they echo every rhythm except this one!
- Give each child a pair of pencils to tap together. Try echoing some tapped pencil rhythms. You can repeat all the word rhythms practised before, (see 5. above), but using pencil pairs. Encourage the children to try and keep together when they echo the rhythms.
- Try tapping the pencils in time to the beat on the floor as you sing songs. This rhythmic accompaniment will help children to keep together and involve children with EAL, even if they don't know the words to the songs.

All rounders

PSED: Introduce special echo clapping patterns as signals for different things, for instance when you want the children to stop what they are doing and listen, or if it is too noisy in the classroom.
CL: Ask children to think of their own ideas of phrases for word rhythms to clap or tap. they can use the 'I like _____' or '_____ are tasty' as helpful frameworks.
M: Try some counting echo clapping and invite children to count how many claps or taps they hear.

Chapter Four: Real rhythms

Clap your name

Try some clapping games to help children with EAL learn each other's names and gain confidence in a large group.

What you need:

- Space and time for echo clapping
- A list of all the children's names
- Puppet
- Simple rhythms to clap
- White boards and pens

What to do:

1. Invite the children to sit in a circle so that everybody can see and hear each other.
2. Start with some echo clapping, see page 26.
3. Play 'Clap, clap, gap, gap'. Start a slow clapping pattern by clapping two times and then marking two silent beats or 'gap' by moving your hands apart. Ask the children to join in with you. Keep the beat really steady.
4. Explain that you are going to ask them to say their name in the two beat gap as you go around the circle. Can you get all the way round without stopping?
5. If children with EAL are shy or reluctant to say their name let the Puppet say it with them and move on around the circle. Check on correct pronunciation for all the children's names.
6. Repeat the game, but this time ask the children to clap the rhythm of their name as they say it. Again let the puppet join in with anybody who is struggling.
7. Help children to identify how many claps their name requires by counting the syllables if necessary.
8. Go round again and this time everybody can say and clap or tap each other's names together.
9. Change the number of claps to three or four and make the gaps longer. Let children take turns to make up or improvise clapping patterns to clap in the gap. If they cannot think what to clap remind them that they can just copy the three or four claps.

Whatever next

- This repeating pattern of claps and gaps also works well for other topics such as weather, food or animals. Children can take turns to insert a word related to the topic in the gap around the circle. Try not to repeat a word that has already been said.
- Introduce a simple rhythm notation using I = one clap II = two quick claps. Ask children to work with talk partners and write their rhythms down on a white board for each other to clap or tap.

All rounders

CL: Learn how to say hello in as many different languages as possible. Invite children with EAL to share the word for 'hello' in their language. Use these words in the 'Clap, clap, gap, gap' game.

PD: Ask children to sit facing their talk partner and try some clapping coordination games. Try this sequence: clap together, clap partners hands, clap together, right hands together, clap together, left hands together, clap together, and so on!

L: Help children to make illustrated name cards to use in the game. Place their names on the carpet in front of them to help children to recognise each other's names and reinforce the learning.

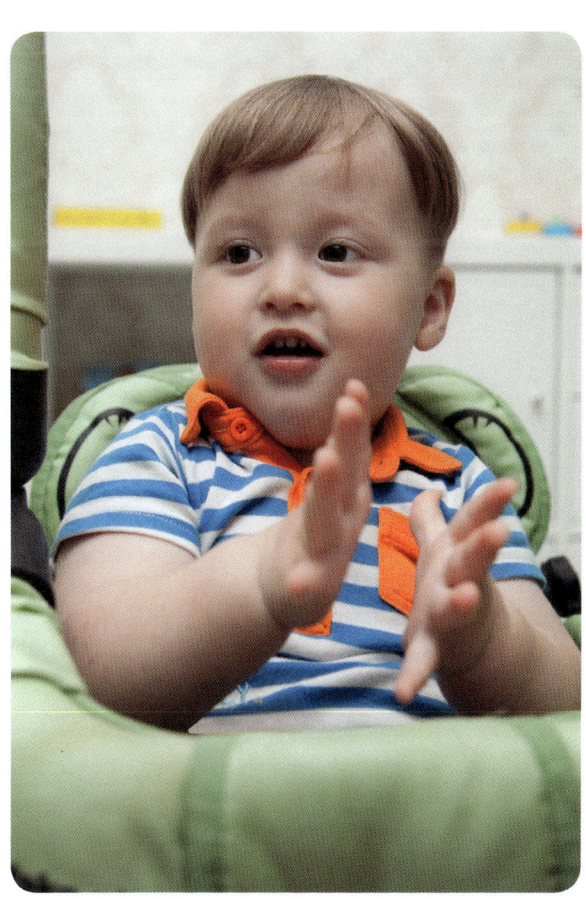

Chapter Four: Real rhythms

Body percussion

Try some rhythm games using different body percussion sounds such as, clapping, tapping, clicking, stamping and children with EAL have less words to worry about!

What you need:

- Space and time for making music
- Tablet or recording equipment
- 'Leader cap'

What to do:

1. Invite all the children to stand in a circle so that everybody can see and hear each other. Make sure children with EAL are next to a supportive talk partner.
2. Start with some echo clapping, see page 26. Ask for volunteers to lead.
3. Introduce some finger tapping and then try hand tapping on different parts of the body - knees, shoulders, head (gently!), thighs, and so on.
4. Ask the children if they know any other types of 'body percussion'. Add stamping, finger clicking, rubbing hands together, and silent nodding to their repertoire.
5. Sing this song to the tune of 'Here we go round the mulberry bush':

This is the way we clap our hands,
Clap our hands, clap our hands.
This is the way we clap our hands,
Making sounds together.

Change the action words to 'stamp our feet', 'click our fingers' or 'slap our knees'.

6. Can they think of any new sounds they can make using their hands? Try clapping with cupped hands, tapping knuckles, tapping finger nails, slapping hands on floor, or banging fists on the table.
7. Make up some simple patterns using two or three different body percussion sounds for children to echo.
8. Ask for volunteers to lead the circle by inventing their own simple pattern. Let them wear the 'Leader cap'. Children must keep copying patterns until the leader takes the cap off and passes it round the circle to the next leader.
9. Play 'Play that again!' Make up a simple pattern using two sounds such as 'clap clap stamp clap'. Ask children to repeat this same pattern over and over. Explain that it then becomes an ostinato or riff.
10. Make it harder by using three or four different body percussion moves in the riff.

Whatever next

- Play 'Riff Diff'. Set up a repeated pattern or riff of moves for children to copy over and over. When you shout 'Riff Diff' the pattern changes and the children have to quickly start to copy the new pattern.
- Film the children playing some of these games using a tablet, phone or camera. Let children watch themselves and make improvements.

All rounders

CL: Make up a story and use body percussion for sound effects. Stamping for footsteps, finger clicks for a ticking clock, tapping for rain drops, and clap with cupped hands for thunder to create the sounds in a spooky story. Record the sound effects.

M: Ask children to work with their talk partner to think of symbols to represent each of the body percussion sounds, for instance:
X = clap, t = tap, * = stamp, + = click.
Can they notate some patterns for their partner to read and repeat?

Chapter Four: Real rhythms

Clap it, tap it, say it, play it

Use word rhythms to make music and develop vocal and rhythmic confidence in all the children.

What you need:

- A list of all the children's names
- White boards and pens
- Pairs of rhythm sticks or claves, enough for each child
- Drums

What to do:

1. Ask children to sit in a circle so that they can see and hear everybody. Make sure children with EAL are next to a supportive talk partner.
2. Start with some echo clapping, see page 26.
3. Remind them of the name game in Clap your name, see page 27. Can they count the syllables in their name and clap the rhythm?
4. Give out instruments so each child has either a pair of claves or a drum in front of them.
5. Introduce the 'clap it, tap it, say it, play it' system.
6. Try clapping the children's names together around the circle. Then repeat tapping them quietly using two fingers on palms of hands. Say the words really loud next time round. And finally play the word rhythms on claves or drums.
7. Use this principle to clap other words. Choose some useful words for all the children to learn, especially children with EAL, such as morning, midday, afternoon, evening, and night. Learn names of meals, the days of the week, the four seasons, months of the year, and so on.
8. Try clapping the word rhythms of the days of the week or the months of the year around the circle. Use the 'clap it, tap it, say it, play it' chant to reinforce learning. Repetition is a great way to help children acquire language and new vocabulary.
9. Think of some other useful words for children with EAL to learn using this game such as question words, words to describe feelings, etc.

Whatever next

- Some children wth EAL will be ready to write down some of the words too. Let them work with a talk partner and use whiteboards and pens to have a go at writing down new words.
- Try some 'Mime it' activities. Children walk around the room and you call out a verb for children to mime until you shout 'freeze'. Try verbal phrases such as 'eating a banana', 'stroking a cat', 'jumping in a puddle' and 'catching a fish'.

All rounders

L: Introduce a 'word of the week' that children can learn to clap, tap, say and play. Make sure the children know how to use the word in a sentence and encourage them to incorporate it into general conversation.

M: Use the 'clap it, tap it, say it, play it' chant to learn to say mathematical signs such add, subtract, multiply and divide, or different shapes - square, circle, triangle, rectangle.

PD: Find other instruments or tools to use to tap rhythms such as pairs of tops from fabric softener bottles or pairs of pencils. Try some dance moves using rhythms.

Chapter Four: Real rhythms

Clave waves

Use pairs of claves or rhythm sticks to echo, tap and improvise rhythms together.

What you need:

- Pairs of rhythm sticks or claves, enough for each child
- Dowelling
- Sandpaper
- Wood varnish
- Two small baskets
- Choosing Hat

What to do:

1. Ask the children to sit in a large circle and place a pair of claves in front of each child.
2. If there are no claves available, make your own using thick dowelling cut into 15-20cm lengths. Smooth the cut ends with sandpaper and varnish the sticks.
3. Show the children how to hold the claves, one in each hand, standing up tall like candles on their knees. This is called 'rest position' because the claves cannot make a sound.
4. Show children how to hold one clave still in one cupped hand and tap it with the other clave making a loud resonant sound.
5. Invite the children to copy some simple rhythm patterns played on the claves - echo tapping. See 'Echo clapping' on page 26 for further ideas.
6. Divide the circle into small groups and challenge the children to copy you group by group. Which group is the best at accurately copying the rhythm and keeping together? Make sure children with EAL are next to a supportive talk partner.
7. Use the Choosing Hat to select children to lead the echo tapping.
8. Play 'Chinese Whispers' on the claves. Try a simple word version first to help children with EAL understand how it works. Pass a pattern round the circle by asking the children to copy their neighbour and try not to change the rhythm as it moves round.
9. Put the claves away using a 'Clave Wave'. Send the two baskets around the circle in opposite directions. Invite each child to place their claves into the basket as it goes round. They must not put their claves away until the person before them has already done so.

Whatever next

- Next time, try using the 'Clave Wave' to give out the claves to the group. Pass the baskets round and ask each child to take out a pair of claves and place them upright on their knees or flat on the floor. Anybody who doesn't resist the temptation to play them has to put them back!
- Try some 'Question and Answer' patterns. Make up a question pattern such as I II I I (tap, tap-tap, tap, tap)? Ask the children to invent an answer pattern that must be different from the question.

All rounders

CL: Use the claves to create sound effects in a rhyme or story. Sing 'Hickory Dickory Dock' and use the claves to play the repeating 'tick tock' sound of the clock. Tap along to 'Peter hammers with one hammer; or 'Cobbler, cobbler, mend my shoe'. Tapping claves make a good sound effect for knocking on the door, donkey's footsteps, raindrops or a woodpecker.

M: Try some claves maths. Invite two children to stand up and hand them a number card face down. Ask the first child to tap the number on their card while the listening children count. Then the second child taps their number. Who can add the two numbers together? Repeat with some simple take away sums.

Chapter Four: Real rhythms

Drumming drills

Try these group drumming activities with a small group of children to develop confidence and rhythm skills.

What you need:

- Large gathering drum or individual drums
- Left and Right stickers

What to do:

1. Place a big gathering drum in the middle of the circle.
2. Sing this call song to the tune of 'Did you ever see a Lassie' and gather a small group of children around the drum. Include some children with EAL in each small group. Alternatively, give each child their own drum or tambour to play.
   If your name is ____, ____, ____,
   If your name is _____,
   Come and play the drum.
3. Invite children to copy rhythm patterns that you tap on the drum. Can they keep together?
4. Choose one of them to be the leader and invent a rhythm for the others to copy.
5. Use Left and Right stickers to help children identify left and right hands. Explain left and right to children with EAL. They may find it easier to use their home language words here.
6. Try some drumming drills using left and right hands: L, R, L, R; L L , R R; or L - R - LRLR. Ask the children to make up some of their own.
7. Play this drum version of 'I hear thunder' (see page 19)
8. Show them how to make loud thunder sounds with the palms of their hands on the drum as they sing the first two lines.
9. Change it to finger tips tapping gently on the drum for the sound of the raindrops in the third and fourth lines.
10. Perform to the rest of the group. Repeat this activity with another small group of children until everybody has had a turn.

Whatever next

- If children are struggling to identify their left and right hands use this trick. Hold up the left hand, index finger and thumb, and show them that it makes an 'L' shape. The right hand index finger and thumb make a 'J'.

- Use the gathering drum or individual drums to accompany other favourite songs and rhymes. Add a drum beat to 'The Grand Old Duke of York' or 'The ants go marching'.
- Try some tempo activities using the strong beat of the drum to set the tempo. Invite the children to stand in a circle and march around in time to the drum. Speed up or slow down and see if they can stay in time. Choose some children to play the drum beat and vary the tempo.

All rounders

PSED: This activity requires a lot of patience and turn-taking amongst the children. Encourage them to listen to each other and support each other's efforts and achievements on the drums.
CL: Read *The Leopard's Drum* by Jessica Souhami. Let the children take turns to play a drum as though it were the most 'magnificent drum' in all the world.
UW: Find out about drums from different countries around the world, such as Djembes from West Africa, Conga from Africa, Tabla from India, Bodhran from Ireland, Bongos from Cuba, Cajon from Latin America and so on. Listen to examples of them being played on YouTube.

Supporting children with EAL in the early years

Chapter Five: Making music

These activities provide children with the opportunity to make music together in pairs, small and large groups, using a variety of different instruments. They can communicate non-verbally and feel part of a significant creative experience which will boost self-esteem and self-confidence.

How to help children with EAL: Making music together helps children with EAL to communicate with each other in an inclusive creative environment as their language skills develop alongside.

You can:
- interact with children as they create musical sounds together
- follow simple hand gestures to include every child in music-making
- devise written or graphic symbols for recording musical ideas.

Chapter Five: Making music

Shake, rattle and ring

Use a selection of different sounding musical instruments in the music corner for all the children to create and change sounds together.

What you need:

- Some instruments to shake - maracas, tambourines, eggs
- Some instruments to rattle - castanets,
- Some instruments to tap - woodblocks, claves, drums,
- Some instruments to scrape - guiro, cabasa
- Some instruments to ring - jingle bells, cowbell, triangle
- Tablet or camera
- Whiteboards and pens
- Cards and felt pens
- Choosing Hat

What to do:

1. Set up a music corner with a selection of different musical instruments for children to handle, explore and play together.
2. Encourage pairs and small groups of children to work in the music corner together. Try to be available to demo instruments where necessary.
3. Let children film each other while making music.
4. Use one word signs to encourage children to explore different ways of playing instruments - shake, rattle, tap, scrape, ring, pluck, blow. Encourage children with EAL to share some of these words in their home language.
5. Make sound cards using graphic patterns for them to interpret: /\/\/\/\ = shake, o o o o = tap 4 times, ////// = scrape, * * * = ringing, and so on.
6. Try some mix and match symbols and let children choose how to interpret them:
   /\/\/\/\ o o o o...or...+ o + o... or.../\./\./\./\ ////// o
7. Invite children to make their own graphic scores or sound patterns using their own symbols for others to read. Practise drawing them on whiteboards and when they are happy with a pattern ask them to copy it onto cards using coloured felt pens.
8. Sit all the children together in a circle and place a selection of musical instruments in the middle.
9. Use the Choosing Hat to select children to play each others' graphic sound patterns.
10. Talk about changing sounds. Can they make some 'thick' or 'thin' sounds? How would that change the graphic score or picture? Try again using a different choice of instruments.

Whatever next

- Provide some tuned percussion instruments such as, xylophones, chime bars, hand chimes, metallophones and boomwhackers and encourage children to explore pitch patterns using these sounds.
- Set up an electronic keyboard in the music corner with headphones so children can explore the different sounds they can make.
- Introduce the word 'timbre' and encourage children to recognise different instrument sounds. Play 'Who said that?' by inviting children to play a sound behind a screen for the others to identify.

All rounders

PSED: Encourage children to play cooperatively in the music corner, taking turns and respecting each other's ideas, needs and feelings.
L: Make some word cards to use alongside the graphic cards so children become familiar with the written words for shake, rattle and ring, etc.
M: Talk about patterns children could use when creating graphic sound cards. Use mathematical language such as next, after, between, before, match, copy, alternate, repeating, names of shapes, etc.
UW: Talk about some of the musical instruments children with EAL are familiar with from home, see 'Sounds of home', page 24.

Chapter Five: Making music

Start and stop

Try some simple conducting activities using hand signs to start and stop the sounds of different musical instruments. Children with EAL may feel more able to communicate using non-verbal signals.

What you need:

- A selection of classroom percussion instruments: maracas, tambourines, triangles, sleigh bells, drums, claves, castanets, cabasas, guiros - one for each child.
- Puppet
- Choosing Hat

What to do:

1. Make sure children have already had lots of opportunities to handle and experiment with instruments (see 'Shake, rattle and ring', page 33).
2. Sit all the children down in a large circle and place an instrument on the floor in front of each child. Try to do this randomly so that no two instruments the same are next to each other.
3. Explain to the children that you are going to use some simple conducting signs for them to follow.
4. Ask them to carefully pick up their instruments and hold them still without making a sound.
5. Show them both hands open with palms facing upwards as a signal to 'start' playing their instruments. Close both hands into fists facing downwards as a signal to 'stop' playing.
6. Practise this lots of times until children can stop very quickly and all at the same time!
7. Ask all the children in the circle to practise the stop and start moves! Help them to exaggerate the moves so they are very clear to the musicians. Demonstrate how not to do it using the puppet!
8. Use the Choosing Hat or ask for a volunteer to conduct the children in starting and stopping the instruments. Children with EAL may feel more confident using hand signs than verbal instructions.
9. Let them walk round the circle starting and stopping individual children so they can hear some solo sounds.
10. Then ask them to combine sounds into duets, trios and quartets (see below).

Whatever next

- Ask the children to think of some new ways to start and stop the sounds. Could they use a specific instrument sound, a clapped rhythm pattern or a different gesture?
- Invite children with EAL to share their home language for 'start' and 'stop'.
- Sort the instruments into groups of similar types of instruments (see 'Play it again Jam', page 35). Ask conductors to try starting and stopping the groups and compare their sounds.

All rounders

CL: Introduce the words solo, duet, trio, and quartet to the children to describe groups of musicians.
PD: Play some physical games that require children to stop really quickly such as 'Sound Statues'. Choose a loud sound or instrument as a signal to stop and create a statue. Invite children to move in different ways around the room until they hear the 'stop' sound.
M: Compare the popularity of five or more musical instruments with the children. Represent the results in a pie chart. Which is the most popular instrument in the group? Which is the least popular. Why?

Chapter Five: Making music

Play it again Jam

An opportunity for all children to make music together and 'jam' in small and large groups using lots of different musical instruments.

What you need:

- A selection of classroom percussion instruments: maracas, tambourines, triangles, sleigh bells, drums, claves, castanets, cabasas, guiros - one for each child.
- A few tuned percussion instruments and beaters
- 4 plastic hoops
- Recording equipment
- Puppet/Choosing Hat

What to do:

1. Make sure children have already had lots of opportunities to handle and experiment with instruments (see 'Shake, rattle and ring', page 33).
2. Sit all the children down in a large circle and place an instrument on the floor in front of each child. Try to do this randomly so that no two instruments the same are next to each other.
3. Try some simple starting and stopping sounds (see 'Start and stop', page 34) until children are really alert and able to start and stop playing all together.
4. Explain that you are going to sort the instruments into groups. You can do this according to how they are played - shake, rattle, tap, scrape or the materials that they are made from - wood, skin, metal, plastic. Just make sure you all agree on which sorting criteria you are using! Make sure the children with EAL understand which sorting criteria you are using.
5. Place the four plastic hoops on the floor in the middle of the circle and ask all the children who are shaking their instrument to come and sit around the first hoop. Ask them to play their sounds together and then carefully place the instrument in the hoop. Repeat with the next type of sound in the next hoop.
6. Ask the children to listen carefully to the sounds of the four hoops. Can they hear the difference between the sounds?
7. Use the Puppet or Choosing Hat to select a group of four children, a quartet, who can each choose an instrument from one of the circles. Ask them to stand in or by the circle and play their chosen sounds, one after the other. Repeat until lots of the children have had a turn playing in a quartet.
8. Explain to children with EAL that to 'jam' in music is another word for improvise or make up on the spot. Ask them to 'Play it again Jam' in a different order. Can the listeners tell what has changed?

Whatever next

- Add a fifth hoop to the sorting circles and include some tuned percussion sounds.
- Extend 'Play it again Jam' to other different ways of playing patterns. Try fast/slow, loud/quiet and long/short variations. Can the listeners tell what has changed? Ask them to suggest some different ways to change the sounds.
- Encourage children to explore 'jamming' together as part of free choice play.

All rounders

PSED: As the children are involved in listening to the different sounds of instruments, encourage them to choose a favourite sound. Which are the group's top five sounds?

M: Add a mathematical element to the activity by asking children to choose how many times they want the sounds repeated, for instance Play it again 4X.

Chapter Five: Making music

Loud and quiet

Develop conducting skills to include dynamics - loud and quiet, and tempo - fast and slow. Help children with EAL to use verbal and non-verbal communication skills.

What you need:

- A selection of classroom percussion instruments: maracas, tambourines, triangles, sleigh bells, drums, claves, castanets, cabasas, guiros - one for each child.
- Puppet
- Choosing Hat

What to do:

1. Start by making the puppet whisper the children's names one by one and ask them to come and sit down in a circle.
2. Talk about different dynamics or volume - loud and quiet. Try singing some nursery rhymes using a quiet or loud voice. Invent signals to indicate which dynamic to use, such as fingers on lips for quiet and hands on ears for loud! Encourage children with EAL to share their ideas for non-verbal signals.
3. Place an instrument in front of each child randomly so that no two same instruments are next to each other.
4. Remind the children of the conducting signs you have been using for 'Start and stop' see page 34. Practise until the children are really quick at following directions.
5. Play 'Quiet as a mouse' and invite each child to make the quietest sound possible on their instrument all the way around the circle.
6. Show the children the conducting sign for 'quiet' which is hands open, palms up, with hands touching. Try some quiet sounds as a large group.
7. If you're feeling brave invite each child to make a contrasting loud sound on their instrument. Emphasise that the instruments can be damaged if they are handled too roughly.
8. Show the children how to change the conducting sign to 'loud' by moving the open hands apart until the arms are outstretched for optimum volume.
9. Use the Choosing Hat or ask for a volunteer to conduct the instruments and introduce some loud and quiet sounds.
10. Ask the children to change the sound gradually from quiet to loud and back again by slowly opening and closing their arms.
11. Can the children think of some ways to change the tempo or speed of their instruments. Repeat some of the above activities contrasting fast and slow playing. Which hand signal could they use to direct fast and slow playing?

Whatever next

- Create some night and day sound pictures by asking the children to choose a selection of suitable quiet sounds for the night and loud sounds for the day. Use both musical instrument sounds and voice and body percussion sounds.
- Invite children with EAL to share their home language for 'loud' and 'quiet'.
- Sort the instruments into groups of similar types of instruments (see 'Play it again Jam', page 35). Ask conductors to try playing loud and quiet sounds with the groups and compare their sounds. Can the drums play quietly? Can the maracas play loudly?

All rounders

CL: Make a collection of other words for 'loud', such as noisy, deafening, thunderous, earsplitting, shouted, yelling, roaring, forte, etc. And 'quiet', such as silent, muted, calm, placid, hushed, tranquil, soft, piano, etc.
UW: Watch some orchestral or choir conductors on YouTube. Can the children see how they help the musicians play loud and quiet sounds? What happens when they want the musicians to play fast or slow?

Chapter Five: Making music

Write your own

Use simple symbols to enable children to write their own musical patterns and sounds. Children with EAL will enjoy inventing graphic symbols.

What you need:

- A selection of classroom percussion instruments: maracas, tambourines, triangles, sleigh bells, drums, claves, castanets, cabasas, guiros - one for each child.
- 4/5 plastic hoops
- Whiteboards and pens
- Strips of card
- Felt pens
- Some tuned percussion instruments
- 5 glass bottles and a jug of coloured water

What to do:

1. Make sure children have already had lots of opportunities to handle and experiment with instruments (see 'Shake, rattle and ring', page 33).
2. Sit all the children down in a large circle and place an instrument on the floor in front of each child. Try to do this randomly so that no two same instruments are next to each other.
3. Sort the instruments into four groups according to the materials they are made of - skin, metal, wood, plastic and place them into four labelled hoops in the middle of the circle (see 'Play it again Jam', page 35).
4. Invite children to come and place their instrument in the correct hoop or group. Help children with EAL who may be uncertain what their instrument is made of.
5. Invent a shortcut symbol to represent each group such as skin = o , metal = △ (triangle), wood = X, plastic = P and make cards showing these symbols for the children to use.
6. Invite children to come out and make a pattern using four symbol cards, for instance: o o X △ or X P X P and let them choose four musicians to go and select an instrument from the corresponding groups and play the pattern. Encourage children to choose different instruments from the groups so that each time it is played the sound will change.
7. Invite children to work with a talk partner and write their own patterns on whiteboards or strips of card.
8. Let children take turns to play each other's music to the group.
9. Place some of the cards in the music corner for children to come back to and play together.

Whatever next

- Can the children think of different ways to vary the sounds, e.g. change they dynamics (loud/quiet) or tempo (fast/slow)?
- Film the children playing their own and each other's music.
- Let children explore writing simple tunes using a tuned percussion instrument set up with a pentatonic or five-note scale of C D E G A. They can use the letter names to write a sequence of notes for each other to play.

All rounders

M: Make a bottle phone using five glass bottles containing different amounts of coloured water. Each one should play a different note when gently tapped with a metal spoon. Arrange them in pitch order, left to right, low to high and label them 1 - 5. Children with EAL can now write musical patterns using numbers.

PD: Play 'Run around sound'. Label each corner of the room with one of the four groups of sounds - skin, metal, wood and plastic. Stand in the middle and play one instrument. Ask the children to run to the appropriate corner. Repeat but hide the instrument behind a screen so the children have to listen.

Supporting children with EAL in the early years

Chapter Six: Exploring colour and patterns

Children can express themselves through a variety of visual art activities without begin restricted by any limitations through their emerging language. Start with simple activities using strong contrasting primary colours and patterns.

How to help children with EAL: As children with EAL are absorbed in different visual art activities they will gain in self-confidence and begin to talk about themselves as they play.

You can:
- explore primary colours in absorbing detail
- organise colour days at your setting for children to share colour activities
- enrich their world by opening their eyes to colour.

Chapter Six: Exploring colour and patterns

Black and white

Start by exploring and talking about specific colours with children with EAL. Use the strong contrast of black and white colours to create some exciting artwork with the children.

What you need:

- White paper and black felt pens
- Black paper and white chalks
- Black and white paint
- A selection of paint brushes
- Black and white paper
- Newspaper
- White art straws
- Scissors, glue
- Snow white play dough
- Camera, tablet

What to do:

1. Introduce the colours black and white to all the children and explain that you are going to try some expressive arts activities using these two colours. Invite children with EAL to share the words for black and white in their home language.
2. Pencils and pens: Start by encouraging children to use different thicknesses of black pens on small pieces of white paper to draw penguins, zebras, pandas, dalmatian dogs, cats and any other black and white animals they can think of.
3. Chalks and pastels: Let children experiment with white chalk on black sugar paper drawing figures, patterns and shapes.
4. Painting: Set up easels with black sugar paper and provide children with white paint and lots of different sizes of paint brushes. Invite children to paint a skeleton figure (see 'Heads, shoulders, knees and toes', page 15).
5. Collage: Use black paper and white art straws to create different cut and stick pictures and patterns.
6. Look at images of newspaper collage on the internet. Let children experiment with tearing or cutting strips and shapes out of black and white newsprint and creating their own collages.
7. Modelling: Make a pâpier maché zebra/pig using small strips of newspaper stuck in layers onto a plastic bottle, using wallpaper paste or flour and water glue. Stick on bottle tops or egg box cartons for legs. Apply several layers of pâpier maché and finish off by sticking on some black sugar paper stripes or spots. Use PVA glue to varnish the finished model.
8. Photography: Encourage children to use the camera or tablet to take some black and white pictures of your setting, inside and outside.

Whatever next

- Show the children some images of artwork by Bridget Riley who produced a range of paintings using black and white in the 1960s called Op-art. How do the children feel when they look at these paintings?
- Let them use black sugar paper, plain white paper, scissors, rulers and glue to cut and stick their own Op-art pattern pictures.

All rounders

PSED: Organise a 'Black and White Day' at your setting. Make sure invitations to special days are available in home languages for parents of children with EAL. Invite children and staff to come wearing black and white clothes, and set out lots of black and white dressing up clothes. Make some black and white badges to wear for those who forget. Decorate the walls with black and white paper chains and black and white fabric or curtains. Play draughts and other games using black and white boards. Display lots of the black and white artworks around for visitors to admire and enjoy.

Chapter Six: Exploring colour and patterns

Seeing red

Explore the colour red with all of the children looking at food, animals, clothes, patterns and artwork.

What you need:

- White paper and red crayons, chalks, pastels, felt pens
- Red and white paint
- A selection of paint brushes
- A selection of red paper and other collage materials
- Red play dough
- Red fruit - strawberries, raspberries, apples, cherries,

What to do:

1. Introduce the colour red to all the children and explain that they are going to be able to choose from lots of different 'red' activities to try.
2. Make a list of the word 'red' in lots of different languages represented by children with EAL in your setting.
3. Pencils and pens: Start by encouraging the children to draw everything that they can think of that is all or partly red. Brainstorm ideas to help them first: tomatoes, strawberries, raspberries, apples, cherries, pomegranates, water melon, chillies, some flowers (poppies, tulips, roses), ladybirds, lips, autumn leaves, robins, foxes, fire extinguishers, fire engine, double decker bus, stop signs/lights, etc.
4. Painting: Set up easels with white paper and provide lots of shades of red paint for children to use. Invite them to choose one red thing from the list above and to paint its picture.
5. Collage: Use different textured and shades of red paper and material to create a collage. Make sure there is shiny red paper, cellophane or sweet wrappers, tissue paper, cardboard, and so on, alongside red materials, wool, netting, faux fur, etc.
6. Try some group 'red' art. Draw the outline of a giant red apple, fire engine or ladybird and invite children to find red paper from photographs in magazines to cut or tear and stick onto the shape.
7. Make red fruit kebabs with the children for snack. Make a selection of red fruit (see What you need) for them to choose from. Show them how to thread them onto a wooden skewer in order to make a repeated pattern.
8. Modelling: Make some red play dough for children to handle and mould. Can they make some red ladybirds? What could they use for spots?

Whatever next

- Show the children images of some Mark Rothko paintings that feature the colour red such as 'Black in Deep Red', 'Four-Darks-in-Red' and 'Reds and Violets over Red'.
- Use a huge piece of paper on the floor and let children cover it with red paint. Use big brushes and sponges. Explore different shades of red. Start from the middle and work outwards otherwise everybody and everything will end up red!

All rounders

PSED: Organise a 'Red Day' at your setting. Make sure invitations to special days are available in home languages for parents of children with EAL. Invite children and staff to come wearing red clothes. Provide red dressing up clothes and accessories for those who forget. Only use red utensils in the home corner. Share red jelly or the red fruit kebabs for snack (see above). Sort out all the red bricks, toys, and equipment for children to play with and put red food colouring in the water tray. Tell them the story of 'Little Red Riding Hood'. Make some red cellophane glasses for children to wear as they look around the world - rose-tinted spectacles!

PD: Make a red stop sign and use it to play some movement games.

Chapter Six: Exploring colour and patterns

Feeling blue

Discover all kinds of the colour blue through drawing, painting, collage, up cycling (see 7. below), and music.

What you need:

- A box of small blue items
- White paper and blue crayons, chalks, pastels, felt pens
- Blue and white paint
- A selection of paint brushes
- A selection of blue paper and other collage materials
- Blue play dough
- Blueberries and pancake ingredients

What to do:

1. Introduce the colour blue to all the children and explain that they are going to be able to choose from lots of different 'blue' activities to try.
2. Make a list of the word 'blue' in lots of different languages represented by children with EAL in your setting.
3. Make a discovery box full of small blue items for children to handle and name. This activity can be repeated with each of the different colours.
4. Pencils and pens: Start by encouraging the children to draw everything that they can think of that is all or partly blue such as blueberries, sky, sea water, bluebells and other flowers, blue jeans, sapphires, eyes, bluebirds, and so on.
5. Painting: Set up easels with white paper and provide lots of shades of blue paint for the children to use. Children can make their own lighter blue by mixing white paint in with blue. Ask them to cover the paper with stripes of different blues to represent the sky and water that meet in the middle. Cut out a boat shape to float on the water. Or add blue fishes to the water and blue birds in the sky.
6. Collage: Provide each child with a fish shape template. Invite them to cut out fish scales from different types of blue paper and collage materials and layer them onto the fish.
7. Ask parents to donate any old blue denim clothes. Cut them up and show children how to make up cycled small mats, bookmarks or purses out of the fabric.
8. Make some blueberry pancakes or muffins to share for snack.
9. Modelling: Make some blue play dough for children to handle and mould. Provide some lego wheels and ask children to make model cars with the dough.

Whatever next

- Show the children images of some blue paintings by Joan Miro, for instance 'Bleu I, II or III', or 'Dancer'. Talk about what they can see in the paintings.
- Let children choose one shade of blue to cover a big piece of paper. Let them stick just two or three other small shapes in red, yellow or black somewhere on their picture. What will they call their blue artwork?
- Listen to 'Kind of Blue' by Miles Davies.

All rounders

PSED: Organise a 'Blue Day' at your setting. Make sure invitations to special days are available in home languages for parents of children with EAL. Invite children and staff to come wearing blue clothes, especially blue denim. Provide blue dressing up clothes and accessories for those who forget. Only use blue utensils in the home corner. Make blueberry pancakes or muffins (see above) and share them for snack. Sort out all the blue bricks, toys, and equipment for children to play with and put blue food colouring in the water tray. Share the rhyme 'Little Boy Blue'. Read *I Love You, Blue Kangaroo* by Emma Chichester Clark.

Chapter Six: Exploring colour and patterns

Mellow yellow

Experience the colour yellow in nature with all of the children and find lots of things to inspire art.

What you need:

- A box of small yellow items
- White paper and yellow crayons, chalks, pastels, felt pens
- Yellow paint
- A selection of paint brushes
- A selection of yellow paper and other collage materials
- Paper plates
- Yellow rubber gloves
- Sunflower seeds
- Yellow play dough
- Bananas

What to do:

1. Introduce the colour yellow to all the children and explain that they are going to be able to choose from lots of different 'yellow' activities to try.
2. Make a list of the word 'yellow' in lots of different languages represented by children with EAL in your setting.
3. Make a discovery box full of small yellow items for children to handle and name. This activity can be repeated with each of the different colours.
4. Pencils and pens: Start by encouraging the children to draw everything that they can think of that is all or partly yellow such as the sun, bananas, sweetcorn, sunflowers, lots of other flowers, rubber ducks, chicks, bees, lemons, peppers, emojis, and so on.
5. Painting: Talk about how yellow makes the children feel. Ask them to paint a yellow picture using any of the yellow ideas (see above).
6. Look at images of different emojis. Provide each child with a paper plate and let them design their own emoji. Which emotion have they chosen to show on their emoji?
7. Collage: Make a giant sunflower collage using petals cut out of yellow rubber gloves stuck around a circle drawn onto some black paper. Fill the centre of the circle with glue and sprinkle on some sunflower seeds.
8. Make some banana splits by adding ice cream and chocolate sauce to a banana cut in half. Let children come up with their own ideas about what else to add to make the dessert even more delicious.
9. Modelling: Use some yellow play dough and let children make lots of pretend food for a mellow yellow tea party.

Whatever next

- Look at images of 'The Sunflowers' painted by Vincent Van Gogh. Do the children like this style of painting.
- Bring in some sunflowers or other yellow flowers in a vase and invite children to make their own picture using crayons, chalks, pastels or paints.
- Listen to 'Yellow' by Coldplay or 'Mellow Yellow' by Donovan.

All rounders

PSED: Organise a 'Yellow Day' at your setting. Make sure invitations to special days are available in home languages for parents of children with EAL. Invite children and staff to come wearing yellow clothes. Provide yellow dressing up clothes, hi-vis jackets, fireman and builder's helmets and other yellow accessories for those who forget or struggle to find anything. Only use yellow utensils in the home corner. Share banana splits desserts for snack (see above). Sort out all the yellow bricks, toys, and equipment for children to play with including yellow construction vehicles in the sand tray and put yellow food colouring in the water tray. Read *Big Yellow Digger* by Julia Jarman. Let the children pretend to be yellow minions from 'Despicable me' and dance along to 'Happy' by Pharrell Williams.

Chapter Six: Exploring colour and patterns

Mixing rainbows

Experiment with mixing the three primary colours together to create some new greens, oranges and purples. Invite children with EAL to share the words for these new colours in their home languages.

What you need:

- Three primary colours, red, blue and yellow
- A selection of paint brushes
- Mixing palettes
- Paper
- A selection of green leaves
- Oranges
- Purple play dough
- Rainbow coloured paints

What to do:

1. Talk about the three primary colours, red, blue and yellow, and the artwork children have already explored using these colours.
2. Remind children of the word for these colours in different languages. Create a colour chart showing the colours and ask children with EAL to help add the colour words in different languages.
3. Explain that they are going to try mixing these colours to see which other colours they can create.
4. Provide some children with blue and yellow paint to mix. Do they know which colour they will make? How many different greens can they create? Make a list or collection of green things - grass, leaves, plants, peas, broccoli, cabbage, beans, apples, pears, sprouts, cucumber, and so on.
5. Go on a 'Leaf Walk' and collect lots of different green leaves. Make an array of the different shades of green leaves. Can the children mix green paints to match the rich variety of greens.
6. Provide some children with red and yellow paint to mix. Do they know which colour they will make? Are there different shades of orange? Make a list or collection of orange things - oranges, carrots, pumpkins, autumn leaves, flowers, goldfish, and so on.
7. Make a collection of different oranges, satsumas, clementines, etc. Cut cross sections of the fruit and let children try printing with them using some of the orange paint they have made.
8. Provide some children with red and blue paint to mix. Can they guess which colour it will make? Make a list or collection of purple things - aubergine, beetroot, grapes, plums, lavender, violets, irises, amethyst, and so on.
9. Make some purple play dough for children to handle and mould into fruit, flowers and vegetables. Add some lavender seeds for fragrance.

Whatever next

- Make a rainbow painting by putting blobs of rainbow coloured paint in a row on one side of a piece of paper. Place a long cardboard tube or ruler into the paint and then move it in arch shape over the paper spreading the colours as you go.
- Go to www.bbc.co.uk/learning/schoolradio/subjects/earlylearning/nurserysongs and sing 'I can sing a rainbow'.

All rounders

M: Talk about favourite colours with the children and do a tally chart to see which is the most popular. Make a colourful pie chart with the children to show which colours are preferred and display on the wall ready for the 'Rainbow Day' (see below).

PSED: Organise a 'Rainbow Day' at your setting and invite children to wear their favourite colour for the day, or as many different colours as possible. Make sure invitations to special days are available in home languages for parents of children with EAL. Provide rainbow ribbons for those who forget. Make some rainbow fruit salad for snack using as many different coloured fruits as possible.

Supporting children with EAL in the early years

Chapter Seven: Using a variety of media and materials

Activities ranging from finger painting, portraits, printing, collage, play dough, clay and sculpture are all included here. There is sure to be something that will capture the imagination of every child so that they can explore their creative potential and express themselves.

How to help children with EAL: Children with EAL may need more support from practitioners or encouragement from their peers to 'have a go'. Give them time, space and opportunity to communicate their ideas.

You can:
- set up an online gallery to display children's artwork
- don't worry too much about finished products, the creative act is in the process
- allow children's ideas to change the direction of a project.

Chapter Seven: Using a variety of media and materials

Fingers and thumbs

Try some fun and energetic painting activities using fingers, thumbs, hands and feet. This simple activity allows children with EAL to join in with their peers confidently.

What you need:

- Shallow trays
- Finger paints
- Felt pens
- Brushes
- Lots of different paper
- Wellington boots
- Ink pads, lipstick

What to do:

1. Sing 'One finger, one thumb, keep moving' to introduce the different painting body parts! Let children with EAL share the names of the parts of the body and try a version in their home language.
   One finger, one thumb, keep moving,   x3
   We'll all be merry and bright.
   One finger, one thumb, one hand, keep moving…,
   One finger, one thumb, one hand, one arm, keep moving…,
   One finger, one thumb, one hand, one arm, one leg, keep moving…,
   One finger, one thumb, one hand, one arm, one leg, one foot, keep moving…,
   One finger, one thumb, one hand, one arm, one leg, one foot, one nod of the head…
2. Start with some finger painting using thick finger paint in shallow trays. Let children experiment with different colours (see 'Mixing rainbows', on page 43) and explore what shapes, patterns and pictures they can make.
3. Suggest they use fingers and thumb prints to create pictures of flowers, animals and people and show how to add stems, legs and facial features using thin felt pens.
4. Try some primary-mix hand prints. Ask children to work with a partner. One child paints their hand red, the other yellow. Print the two hand prints on a piece of paper leaving space in the middle for an orange print! Repeat with some other colour mixes.
5. Move onto rainbow hand prints. Let them paint their hand with a paint brush using lots of different colours. Show them how to press their hand gently onto a piece of paper to make a print. Can they repeat it and make some more prints?
6. Combine fingers and hands to create an autumn tree. Use brown paint and a hand with fingers spread out to make a tree trunk. Let the finger prints be Autumn coloured leaves.

Whatever next

- Let children try some welly prints. Use a roll of lining paper outside and invite children to stand in trays of paint in their wellies and then stamp along the paper. Use lots of different colours. Point out the patterns made by the soles of the boots.
- Get really messy and try some barefoot printing. Place a chair at one end of the paper where the children sit and carefully dip their feet into a tray of paint. Help them to walk along the paper. Finish with a bowl of soapy water to stand and wash their feet clean at the end.

All rounders

CL: Make a fingerprint alphabet by asking the children to print different things starting with each letter. A = ant, B = bee, C = cat, and so on.

M: Let the children use hand prints to help with counting activities. Cut out and mount on card some of their rainbow hand prints. Ask them to label the fingers 1-5, 6-10.

UW: Talk about how everybody has completely unique fingerprints. Explain that the police use them to help solve crimes. Help the children to make a set of fingerprints using lipstick or an ink pad to make a pretend ID card for role-play games.

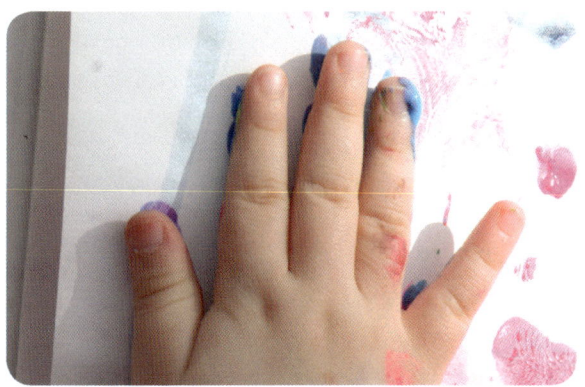

Supporting children with EAL in the early years

Chapter Seven: Using a variety of media and materials

This is me…

Let all the children spend some time looking at themselves in mirrors before producing a variety of self-portraits.

What you need:

- Small hand mirrors
- Pencils, crayons, felt pens
- Easels
- Paper
- Paints
- Palettes
- Brushes
- Magazines
- Camera

What to do:

1. Talk about portraits and self-portraits in art. Show them an example of a self-portrait that you or another adult in the setting have drawn or painted.
2. Start by asking the children to look in the mirror and describe what they see. Remind them of words in different languages to describe facial features, see 'Heads, shoulders, knees and toes', page 15. Talk about different coloured skin tones, eyes and hair colour.
3. Sing this chant as they make observations:
   I look in the mirror, and who do I see?
   I can see me, looking at me!
4. Pencil and pens: Ask children to start by drawing a self portrait using pencils, crayons and felt pens. They can choose to draw just a head and shoulders portrait or their whole body.
5. Painting: Setup easels with large pieces of paper and provide lots of different coloured paints. Encourage children to use palettes to mix the right colour for their skin tone. Again they can choose whether to paint just their head and shoulders or their whole body.
6. Collage: Add a collage effect to their portraits by cutting out pictures of a favourite book, toy, animal, from a magazine and sticking it onto their painting.
7. Make some frames using strips of cardboard decorated with pasta, beads and shiny paper. Alternatively, let each child choose their favourite self-portrait to be displayed and put them all in clip frames.
8. Display the portraits in a self-portrait exhibition called 'This is me…' and invite parents, friends and families to come and visit. Can they identify who the self-portraits were painted by?

Whatever next

- Look at a variety of self portraits by famous artists including Dürer, Kahlo, Van Gogh, Picasso, Matisse, Hockney, and many more. Use some of these to try some portraits in the style of…
- Take some photographs to display next to the children's artwork. Let children take the pictures of each other if possible.
- Try the partner drama game 'Mirrors'. Ask children to work with a partner and call themselves A and B. All the A children are now going to be mirrors and copy everything their partner B says and does when they look in the mirror. Then swap.

All rounders

CL: Ask children to make invitations and posters inviting their families and friends to visit the 'This is me…' exhibition. Make sure invitations to special days are available in home languages for parents of children with EAL.
L: Prepare a catalogue for the self-portrait exhibition. Children can use IT skills to write a simple sentence about their picture or painting.
M: Make a tally list of eye or hair colour in the class. Record the information in a pie chart or bar graph.

Chapter Seven: Using a variety of media and materials

Magic paintings

Show children how to use wax and paint to create magic paintings and send secret messages using signs, symbols and different languages..

What you need:

- White paper
- White candles or pale wax crayons
- Different-coloured thin paint washes
- Paint brushes
- Multi-coloured wax crayons or oil pastels
- Thick paper cut into small sheets
- Black acrylic paint
- Small sticks or cotton buds

What to do:

1. Show the children a 'one I made earlier' example of this style of painting to start the activity. Show them how to make a picture, or one or two familiar words that emerge from the paper as if by magic.
2. Explain to children with EAL that these are called magic paintings.
3. Provide a sheet of white paper and ask them to draw a circle on it using a white candle or pale coloured wax crayons. The circle will be invisible at first.
4. Then show them how to apply a thin wash of paint on top of the circle. The wax resists the paint and the drawn circle appears.
5. Let children draw their own designs on the paper. They can draw fishes and other sea creatures. Use a thin blue wash to watch them emerge from the water. Alternatively, draw birds that suddenly appear flying in the blue sky.
6. Ask children to paint a scene through a window of a garden or street. Add stars and a moon in the sky. Apply a dark blue wash so the scene looks like the night time.
7. Invite children to write their names using the wax crayon. They can use a different colour wash to reveal their magic writing.
8. Can they write or draw a secret message to a friend using this wax resist magic painting? They can use words, drawings or magic symbols.
9. Display some of the magic paintings on the wall. Make fancy frames using cardboard, dried pasta, and gold or silver spray paint.

Whatever next

- Make the pictures even sweeter by using a sugar wash created with coloured food gel or icing, mixed with granulated sugar and warm water to make a shiny, glossy paint. This paint also works when painted onto slices of white bread. All good enough to eat!
- Try some scratch resist art. Ask children to cover a piece of thick paper with stripes of coloured wax crayon or oil pastels. Show them how to press hard and make the colours look strong and thick. Make sure there are no white gaps left.
- Paint over the colours with a layer of black paint.
- Scratch a picture or design through the wet paint using toothpicks, cocktail sticks, matchsticks or cotton buds. Firework shapes work very well in this medium.

All rounders

CL: Talk about other kinds of codes or secret messages such as morse code, braille or ATBASH which is simply the alphabet backwards so A = Z, etc. Can the children make up their own code and write some coded messages?

L: Provide some invisible ink pens and let children write their own secret messages.

M: Ask children to write some number puzzles or sums using the magic paintings or write numbers or shapes using the scratch resist methods.

Chapter Seven: Using a variety of media and materials

Print and press

Let all of the children explore how to print pictures and patterns with different natural and man-made materials.

What you need:

- Different paper
- Paper bags
- Lining paper
- A variety of printing materials: shapes, corrugated cardboard, corks, potatoes, fruit and vegetables, lego bricks, cotton reels, combs, dominoes
- Stamps or printing blocks
- Bubble wrap
- Sponges
- Rolling pins, sponge rollers
- Shallow trays
- Paints

What to do:

1. Lots of different things can be used to print. Explain the terms print and press to children with EAL. Set up a print and press table with shallow trays of paint and a basket full of different items such as corks, bricks, and plastic shapes for children to experiment with by pressing them into the paint and then onto paper.
2. Try some potato printing. Cut a potato in half and carve shapes out of the cut edge. Start with geometric shapes and patterns. Show children how to press the potato, cut side down into the paint tray and then press onto the paper.
3. Try some different fruit and vegetables. Oranges and lemons make lovely patterned prints. Carrots can print circles and rectangles depending on how they are cut. Print with broccoli to make tree shapes and okra to create flowers. Put holders in the ends of sweet corn, roll them in paint, and roll on the paper.
4. Sponges can also be used to print. Cut shapes out of the sponges and use them to print on plain paper bags or paper to use for wrapping parcels.
5. Let children use a mixture of items such as sponges, cardboard tubes, and corks to print a repeating pattern on some lining paper to create fancy wall paper.
6. Print with lego bricks. Print a wall for Humpty Dumpty to sit on. Draw the shape of a house and print a house of bricks for the third little pig.
7. Cover some stamps with bubble wrap and print bubble pictures on a long strip of paper.
8. Cover rolling pins or sponge rollers with bubble wrap, corrugated card, or textured paper and let children print with the rollers on large pieces of paper.

Whatever next

- Let children experiment by finding new things to print with. Fix seven pencils with rubbers on the end together with an elastic band. What happens if they dip the ends in paint and print with them?
- Print with some natural materials such as feathers, flowers, leaves, and stones.
- Print with kitchen utensils - potato mashers, forks, apple corers, spatulas, scrubbing brushes, etc.
- Try some string printing. Use a small cardboard box or a block of wood. Cover one side with glue and attach pieces of string. Make shapes and swirls. Dip the block into a tray of paint and print some patterns.

All rounders

CL: Use some edges of cardboard boxes or lengths of string to print Initial Letters.
L: Print names, words and messages using plastic letters onto strips of paper.
M: Try some simple number sentences by printing with dice. Press dice gently into a sponge soaked in paint and then press onto the paper.
PD: Try some finger, hand or foot prints onto a length of lining paper, see 'Fingers and thumbs', on page 45.

Chapter Seven: Using a variety of media and materials

Family trees

This is a fun and creative activity to encourage all of the children to talk about their friends and families.

What you need:

- Details of families, siblings and grandparents
- Photographs
- Gingerbread man cutters
- Twigs, branching sticks
- Paper, pencils, felt pens, rulers
- Hole punch, string
- Scissors
- Laminator

What to do:

1. Show children a simple family tree of your own or images of family trees online to introduce the activity.
2. Explain that you are going to start by making a friendship tree of all the children in the class. Invite them to draw a small picture of themselves in black ink on white paper. Cut these out and laminate them.
3. Bring a large branch inside or go outside and find a suitable tree. Help children to punch a hole in the top of their picture and use string to hang it onto the tree. This is a good bonding activity to do at the start of term when children are just getting to know each other.
4. Work with children in small groups to talk about their families. How many brothers and sisters do they have? What are their names? How old are they? Use any info you have collected from parents, for example siblings' names, grandparents and other family members.
5. Be sensitive to children who have unconventional family situations. Invite keyworkers to talk to parents of children with EAL to gather information for the family trees.
6. Ask them to draw a picture of themselves, or use a photograph, or draw around a gingerbread man cutter in the middle of a piece of paper. Let them decorate the outline so it looks more like them by adding facial features and favourite clothes.
7. Show them how to draw lines using rulers to connect themselves to any siblings, and to parents and grandparents. Ask them to draw pictures of their family members or write names.
8. Encourage children to talk about their families to each other and to the wider group using their family tree pictures.

Whatever next

- Compare names used for grandparents from different nationalities - granny, granddad, nana, pap, nanny, pops, oma, oupa, babushka, and so on.
- Photograph or film the children sharing their family trees with the group.
- Create an inside 'friendship tree' using handprints made by all the children in different Autumn colours. Cut them out and stick the handprint leaves onto a large tree trunk.

All rounders

PSED: Children need to show sensitivity to others' needs and feelings as they work together and learn about each other's families. Be extra sensitive to children with EAL who have family members in other countries who they might not see very often.
L: There are lots of opportunities for children to write their own names and the names of their family members on the family tree and practise their writing skills.
UW: Talking about their families is an important part of Understanding the World.

Chapter Seven: Using a variety of media and materials

Mini-me models

Children can use different malleable materials to create models of themselves and their friends. Talking to children with EAL while they are involved in playing with dough is very rewarding.

What you need:

- Play dough ingredients
- Salt and flour dough
- Dough or clay tools
- Glass beads, buttons, googly eyes
- Garlic or dough press
- Gingerbread man cutters
- Variations to add to dough: oats, glitter, lavender seeds, sequins
- Scissors
- Camera

What to do:

1. Make some play dough with the children. Mix together 1 cup of plain flour, 1 cup of water, 1/2 cup of salt, 1 tablespoon of cream of tartar, 1 tablespoon of vegetable oil, a few drops of food colouring and heat slowly in a sauce pan until it blends in to a dough. Knead until smooth, leave to cool and store in a ziplock bag or airtight container.
2. Let children have lots of opportunity to experiment and engage in free play with the play dough.
3. Make some different types of play dough by adding some of the variations suggested above. Try different textures by adding oats or sand. Use perfumes to make the dough smell different. Remind children not to eat the dough even if it smells tasty!
4. Make some natural non-coloured play dough for children to make 2D faces. Provide laminated mats with face shapes on them. Let them use glass beads, buttons and googly eyes to create faces. Use coloured dough to create hair by pressing it through a garlic press or dough press to make thin strands.
5. Roll some pink or brown dough to a thickness of 5mm and let children use gingerbread men cutters to make themselves. Can they make the other members of their family or some friends?
6. Ask children to try some 3D mini-me models using balls of dough for heads, egg shape for body and sausages for arms and legs. How can they make it look more like themselves?
7. Arrange the mini-me models in different postures for a display. Can they make their model run, sit, lie?

Whatever next

- Make some salt and flour dough by mixing together 1 cup of plain flour with 1 cup of salt and 1 cup of warm water. The flat models above will work with this dough and can be cooked in a very low oven so that they can be glazed or painted.
- Some of these activities will work with clay as well.
- Watch a film of 'Morph' on YouTube to help inspire children with their mini-me models. Morph even has his own website www.amazingmorph.com

All rounders

PSED: Play dough activities are also an excuse to be very sociable. Children with EAL enjoy sitting together around the table as they play and many opportunities to observe and engage them in conversation arise.
CL: Encourage children to use their mini-me models as characters in made up stories or retellings of traditional stories that they already know.
UW: Help children to observe the changes in state when making the play dough together.

Chapter Seven: Using a variety of media and materials

Clay tiles

Use lots of control and coordination, handling tools to create clay tiles and decorate them with different materials and techniques.

What you need:

- Air dry or kiln fired clay
- Small pots of water
- Clay tools
- Rolling pins
- Cutters
- Matchsticks, lolly sticks, blunt pencil
- List of children's names
- Shiny paper
- Scissors
- Felt

What to do:

1. Children benefit from lots of experience handling clay before making specific things. It is also a social activity so try to provide opportunities for children with EAL to use clay in free play activities.
2. Show children how to make a basic tile by rolling the clay out to a thickness of 5mm and cutting out the shape using a cutter or free hand.
3. Let them choose how to decorate the tile using textured patterns applied with clay tools or a sticks. Help them to write their name on the tile by scratching the letters into the clay.
4. Create a 3D effect on a tile by cutting out smaller pieces of clay and sticking with slip, which is a combination of clay and water. Try making faces by cutting out an oval shape, scratching the eyes and then applying 3D lips, nose, ears and hair!
5. Try some other 3D decorated tiles by cutting out flowers or other shapes and sticking them onto the tile with slip.
6. Make mosaic tiles by sticking small pieces of shiny coloured paper into the clay while it is wet and creating different patterns and shapes.
7. Make a clay drinks mat by cutting a circle or square out of rolled clay, decorating it with clay tools, and painting when dry. Stick a shape cut out of felt on the bottom to make it more steady.
8. Find an autumn leaf. Press it into the rolled out clay and carefully cut round the shape with a knife. Peel off the leaf and it will have left an impression where all the veins pressed into the clay. Paint with autumn colours when dry.

Whatever next

- Try some 3D modelling activities. Make a tea light holder by rolling the clay into a ball, pushing a tea light into the soft clay to make a hole, decorating with patterns and painting when dry.
- Let children try sculpting the clay into different animals shapes. Try making model hedgehogs by adding matchsticks or cut straws for spines or fantasy monsters using pipe cleaners for wings and horns.
- Many of theses activities will also work with play dough or salt and flour dough (see 'Mini-me models', page 50)

All rounders

PSED: Make a birthday cake out of clay to use with the children on their birthdays. While the cake is still wet push 5 candles in to make holes. Paint the cake when dry. Let the children count the candles into the clay cake when it is their special day. Don't forget to sing 'Happy Birthday'.
M: Ask the children to make some snakes by rolling the dough into long lengths or sausages. Can they use rulers to discover who has made the longest or shortest snake?

Chapter Seven: Using a variety of media and materials

Cool collage

Children can use a variety of materials, tools and techniques to create different types of collages. Encourage children with EAL to talk about their collages.

What you need:

- Lots of different materials: paper, card, cellophane, shiny paper, tissue paper, wrapping paper, greetings cards, wall paper, bubble wrap, foil
- Fabric: netting, cotton, faux fur
- Add-ons: sequins, buttons, dry pasta, beads, matchsticks
- Natural materials: shells, sticks, leaves, dried flowers, feathers
- Magazines to cut up
- String, artstraws, wool, wire
- Glue, scissors, hole punch

What to do:

1. All children benefit from the opportunity to explore collage materials in a free play environment so allow lots of time and space for this to happen before trying any more organised activities.
2. Set up a craft table or workshop where all the collage materials are easily accessible so children with EAL can visit and get creative during the day.
3. Try using some shape templates for collage work. Provide children with cardboard templates of bears, dinosaurs and other animals, and ask them to make a collage animal using lots of different paper and fabric.
4. Make a collage meal by cutting out lots of different food shapes or pictures of food from magazines and sticking them onto a paper plate.
5. Provide templates of geometric shapes and invite children to cover them with different materials in particular colours, for instance make a red triangle or blue circle.
6. Ask children to create a collage picture of a garden. They can cut pictures from plant catalogues, add flowers cut out of paper, and use some natural materials. Can they make a garden gate out of matchsticks or a pond from shiny blue paper?
7. Make a stained glass window from black sugar paper and tissue paper. Use a classic arch shape or a star. Hang in the windows to catch the sun on display.

Whatever next

- Picasso was one of the first artists to use the term 'collage'. Show the children his collage online - 'Guitar' (1913). Look at the different materials he used to create this picture: wallpaper, newspaper, cardboard. Ask the children to choose a musical instrument to inspire a collage. Provide templates to help the children use some musical shapes.
- Look at the work of some other famous collage artists online. Look at 'Untitled' (Quality Street), 1943 made out of sweet wrappers. Ask the children to create their own collage using sweet wrappers and packaging.
- Let the children make a collage face using cut up photographs from magazines inspired by the work of Hannah Hoch who originated 'photomontage', see 'German Girl', 1930.

All rounders

PSED: In small groups, ask children to play a game of 'Picture consequences' and see how many strange combinations of collage style characters they can create by taking turns to draw.
M: Encourage children to spend time sorting the collage materials and tidying them into their containers after working in the craft workshop.
UW: Organise a display or exhibition of the different collage artwork and invite parents, families and friends to visit.

Chapter Seven: Using a variety of media and materials

Skilful sculptures

Try using different materials such as sticks, string, stones, and wire to create sculptures inspired by famous artists.

What you need:

- Sticks, twigs, lolly sticks, straws, match sticks
- Fabric, wool, googly eyes
- Stones, rocks, pebbles
- String, nylon twine
- Cardboard
- Wire, pipe cleaners
- Aluminium foil
- Plastic or cardboard shapes
- Metal coat hanger
- Small pieces of soft wood
- Hammers, saw, nails, sandpaper

What to do:

1. Introduce the idea of sculpture to children with EAL as carving or shaping two or 3D forms out of wood, plaster, clay and other materials.
2. Make some stick people out of found twigs or sticks, straws and fabric. Create faces using googly eyes, felt pens and woollen hair. Make families of different-sized stick people.
3. Try twisting pipe cleaners into the shape of a person or figure. Make a circle for the head, and then add one pipe cleaner for the arms and join on another for the legs.
4. Show the children images of Giacometti's sculptures of figures online, for instance 'The Pointing Man' or 'The Cat'. Talk about the thin stick-like limbs. Show children how to cover their pipe cleaner figures with aluminium foil to create mini walking or pointing statues. Can they make a pipe cleaner cat?
5. Look at images of stone art by Carl Peverall. Place lots of different rocks, stones and pebbles in the sand tray and encourage children to try creating balances and sculptures with the stones. Can they build a 'stone man'?
6. Make a hanging mobile inspired by Alexander Calder. Look at images of his work online. Cut out some geometric shapes out of coloured plastic or cardboard. Make holes in them using a hole punch. Hang them onto a metal coat hanger using string or twine.

Whatever next

- Set up a carpentry workshop and show children how to use wood tools such as hammers and saws safely. Use sandpaper to smooth wood to avoid getting splinters. Show them different techniques to join pieces of wood together using nails, screws and string.
- Let children experiment with all the different materials they have used in these activities to create their own individual sculptures.
- Photograph and film the children at work. Display the photographs next to the finished artworks.

All rounders

PSED: Hold an exhibition of the children's sculptures. Invite parents, families and friends. Make sure invitations to the exhibition are available in home languages for parents of children with EAL.
CL: Read *Stick Man* by Julia Donaldson. Ask the children to use the stick people they have made to retell the story. Make up their own stories about Stick people and Stone people.
L: Ask children to produce labels for each artwork including a title and their name. Work together as a group to compile a brochure for the exhibition.

Chapter Eight: Construction workers

Making models in the workshop from a rich variety of different materials provides a stimulating learning environment for many children. Try to keep the workshop well-stocked with junk materials, offcuts of wood, nails and safe carpentry tools, paper and collage materials, plastic and metal lids, glue, tape, string and scissors. Add unusual items regularly to inspire children's imagination.

How to help children with EAL: Try to partner children with EAL with supportive friends who will work with or alongside them in the workshop.

You can:
- encourage individual and group activities
- allow regular access to the workshop during free play
- hold 'shows' for children to display and talk about their models.

Chapter Eight: Construction workers

In the workshop

Encourage children to use lots of recycled materials to create small and large-scale junk models.

What you need:

- Different-sized cardboard boxes, tubes, plastic trays, and other junk materials
- A variety of paper and collage materials: shiny paper, strips of card, tissue paper, sweet wrappers, fabric, dried pasta, glitter, etc.
- Plastic and metal lids, buttons, sticks,
- Glue, sticky tape, stapler, string, paper clips, split pins, hole punch
- Scissors

What to do:

1. Set up a well-equipped workshop in your setting and encourage children to regularly access the area to practise construction skills including joining materials together and creating their own models.
2. Provide easily accessible containers sorted into different-sized boxes, cardboard tubes, plastic trays and packaging, lolly sticks, matchsticks, straws, buttons, collage materials, etc. Encourage children to tidy up after working in the workshop so that items remain sorted and don't get too mixed together.
3. Set up a tape station with lots of different coloured tape, Sellotape, masking tape, on a pole for children to use.
4. Introduce useful construction words such as make, build, connect, join, assemble, hole, slot, fit, cut, stick, glue, tape, string, decorate, push and pull. Help children with EAL to fully access the workshop by explaining all these terms.
5. Once children have spent time freely exploring the resources, set some simple basic challenges such as 'join together three different items', 'build a tall tower', and 'make a decorated box'.
6. Challenge children to make a specific model using just one box - a mobile telephone, Walkie Talkie, or communicating device of some kind. Let children use their finished models in role play activities.
7. Invite children to work with a partner to create a model machine together. Can they tell you what their machine does? Challenge them to make part of their machine move using wheels, string, paper clips or split pins.
8. Work as a group to create a giant machine. Read *Robot Rumpus* by Sean Taylor or another robot story. Involve a small group of children, including children with EAL, to build a robot or time machine together. Use as many of the children's own ideas as possible.

Whatever next

- Make a list of machine sound words - buzz, boing, ding, tick, bang, etc. Encourage children to choose parts of their machines to make different sounds and present their 'Noisy machines' to each other.
- Read or watch some of the *Bob the Builder* stories. Sing the songs. Look at the different machines he uses and make some changes and improvements to the model machines.

All rounders

CL: Make up some stories for the robot or machine made by the children. Help the children to think of a name for their model machine. What adventures will it enjoy? Will it cause trouble somewhere?
PD: Try some movement activities using machine moves and sounds. Ask children to work with a partner and each choose a repeated sound and movement to perform together. Join the pairs into a giant group moving machine.
M: Introduce some mathematical language where appropriate to describe shapes of items such as square, rectangle, circle, triangle, cube, cylinder, pyramid, etc.

Chapter Eight: Construction workers

Miniature model town

Build a model map of your setting and local environment using materials from the workshop.

What you need:

- Lots of different sized cardboard boxes
- Black sugar paper
- Chalks
- Lego bricks, corrugated cardboard
- Scissors
- Glue, sticky tape
- Access to workshop
- Google maps
- A list of children's addresses
- Photographs of children's homes

What to do:

1. Explain to the children that you are going to create a model of your local street, village or town based on a map. Encourage children with EAL to share pictures of their home town if appropriate.
2. Start by looking at your school and local environment on Google maps, street view. Point out local landmarks, shops and special buildings and find the school or setting.
3. Go for a walk around the school and the local streets to note particular buildings and features that could be included in the model.
4. Use resources from the workshop, see 'In the workshop', on page 55, to make model buildings.
5. Ask the children to bring in a photograph of their home. Let them make models of their own houses using junk materials. Help them to cut out shapes for windows. Can they include special features on their models such as the colour of the door, the number or name of the house, the correct number of windows, and so on?
6. Make roofs using folded cardboard. Print brick and tile shapes onto walls and roofs using lego bricks and strips of corrugated cardboard.
7. Make road layouts to place the houses on using strips of black sugar paper with white lines drawn on in chalk.
8. Work together to make models of the school and any other local buildings such as churches, shops, offices, etc. and place them on the map to create a 3D model town.
9. Display the model for visitors to see.

Whatever next

- Are there any natural features near the school to include in the model, such as parks, rivers, gardens, fields, woods, and so on? Can the children think of different ways to create these to add to the model?
- Ask children to make some model cars and people to add to the street scene.
- Let children who have gardens at home paint pictures of them including different plants, trees, and play equipment, etc. Try making collage gardens (see 'Cool collage', p.52).

All rounders

PSED: As the children work together to build this model, help them all to take account of one another's ideas about how to organise the activity.
CL: Encourage children to learn their addresses so they can tell you where they live on the model. Let them use the photographs of their homes and write their own label with the address on to add to the display.
UW: This is a good activity for children with EAL to learn about their new home environment and how it differs from other places where they have lived.

Chapter Eight: Construction workers

Musical medleys

Use a variety of materials from the workshop to make some recycled musical instruments.

What you need:

- Junk materials suitable for making musical instruments such as plastic bottles, plastic cups or yoghurt pots, empty baby milk or sweets tins, cardboard tubes, paper plates, tissue boxes, etc.
- Fillings for shakers - rice, lentils, beans, coins, sand, pebbles
- Elastic bands
- Access to the workshop

What to do:

1. Ask the children to sit in a circle and try some games using musical instruments, see 'Shake, rattle and ring', on page 33, or 'Start and stop', on page 34.
2. Talk about how the different instruments make a sound - shake, rattle, scrape, tap, blow, pluck, etc.
3. Replace the instruments with a pile of junk materials from the workshop and challenge children to explore making sounds with the different items. When they have experimented and got some ideas let them go to the workshop and have a go at making their own musical instruments.
4. Here are some ideas to get you started. **Shakers:** Let them partially fill small clear plastic bottles with fillings to create shakers or maracas. How will the different fillings affect the sound of the shaker? Use glue to secure the lids, so the contents don't spill everywhere.
5. Make some pairs of matching shakers. Put a small amount of filling into the bottom of one opaque yoghurt pot or plastic cup. Turn a second pot or cup upside down on top and tape the two together.
6. Make some **Rain sticks:** Use long cardboard tubes, secured at one end. Push cocktail sticks through the sides of the tube to make obstructions and fill with a handful of rice or lentils. Add a lid and tip the tube up and down to hear the rain falling.
7. **Scrapers:** Use large plastic bottles with ridged sides to create scrapers or guiros. Use a wooden spoon or pencil to scrape along the ridges. These instruments could also have some filling in them so they can be shaken and scraped.
8. Make some **Tin drums:** Use empty baby milk or sweet tins. Use different-sized balloons to create drum skins stretched over the open edges of the tins. Secure them with elastic bands.
9. **Box guitar:** Stretch different-sized elastic bands over an empty tissue box. Can the children pluck them and make different sounds.

Whatever next

- Explain the word medley (a mixture) to the children with EAL and let them use their instruments to create some musical medleys together.
- Play 'String along'. Make sure you have pairs of instruments that make the same sound. Place a set of sounds in the middle of the circle, and a matching set behind a screen. Invite children to go and play one sound behind the screen for the others to copy. Try to play a 'string' or sequence of sounds. Next, ask a child to play two sounds for another child to copy. Keep adding sounds to the sequence. How long a string of sounds can they remember?

All rounders

CL: Encourage children to use their home made instruments to accompany some songs and rhymes.
PD: Go on a walk and find some natural materials to use inside shaker bottles such as leaves, conkers, acorns, pebbles, feathers, sand and water.

Chapter Eight: Construction workers

Memory boxes

Use this unusual art form to help all of the children share ideas, feelings, memories and facts about themselves.

What you need:

- A selection of small trays
- Shallow boxes such as chocolates
- Plastic chocolate or biscuit trays
- Different types of paper
- Wrapping paper, newspaper, wallpaper
- Magazines, greetings cards
- Found objects: stones, pebbles, shells, twigs, leaves
- Small toys
- Glue, tape, string
- Scissors

What to do:

1. Show the children images of Joseph Cornell's collage boxes or 'memory boxes' online. Explain that he used objects that he found, or pictures that reminded him of things, to make his boxes.
2. Go on a walk outside your setting and let children collect some small natural objects such as stones, leaves, twigs, bark, shells, etc.
3. Provide each child with a shallow tray or box to fill with special things.
4. Let them line their boxes with wrapping paper, newspaper or pages from comics and magazines.
5. Add old tickets, photographs, and handwritten words.
6. Cut out pictures from magazines or greetings cards to place in the boxes. These can be mounted on a folded cardboard spring to add a 3D effect.
7. Add a few natural found objects from the walk, if available.
8. Let children choose one or two small items, such as plastic cars, erasers, figures, bricks, balls, pompoms, dried flowers, and so on, to represent their interests and memories. Explain to children with EAL that they can choose any items they like to put in their memory boxes.
9. It is important to ensure that the children experiment with the layout several times until they are satisfied with the effect before anything is stuck down.
10. Alternatively, the activity can be a temporary artwork that is created on a tray, photographed, talked about and then disassembled.

Whatever next

- Invite the children to show their boxes to the group and tell them why they chose the different items. Make sure you make one of your own to show the children.
- Can they invent a story to go with the box and its treasures? Invite EAL children to work with a talk partner and make up a narrative.
- Photograph or film the children creating and talking about their memory boxes.

All rounders

PSED: Children need to show sensitivity to others' needs and feelings as they work together and hear about each other's experiences.
L: Let children choose a few significant words or sentences to write on a piece of paper to add to their memory boxes. Can they sign their name at the bottom of the box like an artist?
M: Use the chocolate plastic trays as counting trays and let children place an object in each section as they develop counting skills.
UW: Encourage children to talk about past experiences and memories as they share their memory boxes.

Chapter Eight: Construction workers

Paper crafts

Take some paper or thin card and try some folding, cutting and sticking activities to make a puppet, a hat or a plane.

What you need:

- Different types of paper: newspaper, A4 coloured sheets, thin card
- Felt pens
- Scissors, hole punch
- Glue, string, paperclips, split pins

What to do:

1. Introduce the art of folding paper - origami. Show children some examples that they can handle or pictures online. Go to www.origami-instructions.com/origami-for-kids.html
2. Start with a very simple puppet. Ask the children to follow all these steps. Take a piece of A4 paper and fold it into 3 lengthways.
3. Fold it in half bringing the two short ends together. Then fold the two short ends back away from the centre fold to create a W shape.
4. Put your thumb in the lower open end and fingers in the top so you can operate the puppet mouth.
5. Draw a face on the top with big eyes, eyebrows, ears, nose, hair, etc. Add a tongue and teeth inside the middle opening. What is their puppet going to say?
6. Fold a sheet of newspaper into a hat. Take a folded sheet of a small newspaper with the fold at the top and fold it in half again, short edges together.
7. Unfold and take each of the top corners down to meet the crease creating a triangle shape.
8. Fold up the bottom edge on each side to make a hat. Decorate and model for each other.
9. Let children experiment with cutting and folding paper to see what they can create. Show them a few simple ideas such as paper lanterns or snowflakes.
10. Try some different cutting and folding techniques including fringing, curling (using the edge of scissors), quilling, and concertina fans.
11. Demonstrate some different joining techniques using glue, hole punch, paperclips, split pins, etc.
12. Invite children to work with a partner and construct the tallest paper tower they can make together.

Whatever next

- Challenge the children to make a paper plane using their own folding ideas and find out which plane flies the furthest. Set up a fair test outside to discover the champion plane designer.
- Let the children choose some other origami folding to try from the website.

All rounders

PSED: Show children how to make a simple pop-up card for birthdays or other special occasions. Fold a piece of A4 paper in half and then half again. Then unfold the paper, and make a fold lengthways. Make a single cut into this fold and fold each side of the cut down into a tiny triangle. When you fold the card up again this should look like a beak or a mouth and can be decorated accordingly!

CL: Let children with EAL work with a confident partner and practise having a conversation using their paper puppets. Invite children to show off their puppets chatting to the rest of the group.

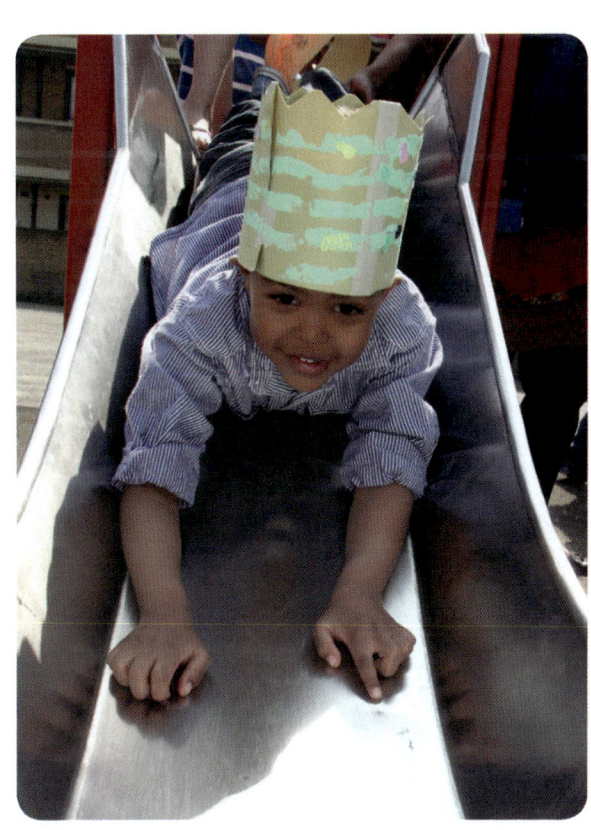

Chapter Nine:
Movement and dance

Encourage all the children to express their ideas, thoughts and feelings through movement and dance activities. Try simple follow-my-leader games with a minimum of verbal instructions and move on to more imaginative dance ideas.

How to help children with EAL: The freedom of expression through movement and dance activities can release some of the tension of language learning for children with EAL.

You can:
- use copying and modelling moves rather than complex instructions
- try to use the children's own ideas when creating dance moves
- share some yoga ideas so children can practise at home.

Chapter Nine: Movement and dance

Somebody says

Play some dramatic music and movement games for children with EAL to use expressive non-verbal gestures and develop concentration.

What you need:

- A big space to move about in
- Music
- Carpet tiles

What to do:

1. Start with some simple follow-my-leader activities. Invite the children to stand in a long line and follow you round moving in different ways - walking, running, hopping, skipping, sliding, jumping, waving arms, etc. Children with EAL will learn by copying their peers.
2. Play a game of 'Simon says' and explain to the children that they must only follow the instructions or copy the actions if you say 'Simon says' first. Try actions such as 'jump up and down on the spot' or 'touch your toes', and dance moves such as 'point your toes' or 'spin around'. Add some more dramatic gestures such as 'salute' or 'jazz hands' or 'pretend to cry'. Children who are out can help spot others.
3. Let children take turns at being the leader and use their names instead of Simon.
4. Play 'Grandmother's footsteps' with the children. Choose a child to be 'Grandmother' who stands facing the wall. All the other children try to creep up to touch her. At any point, Grandmother can turn round and see if she can spot anybody moving. Any children she notices have to go back to the beginning and start again.
5. Change Grandmother to a 'Sleeping lizard' or a 'Tired teacher'. Can the children sneak past without waking them up? Ask them to pretend that the floor they are crossing has turned into a swamp, or is covered in treacle. Will they move in different ways?
6. Play 'What's the time Mr Wolf?' and see how close the children can get to Mr Wolf as he calls out the times and they move the corresponding number of steps nearer. At anytime Mr Wolf can decide it's dinnertime and then he has to try and catch someone to take over as the wolf.
7. Try some musical games, such as 'Musical bumps' or 'Musical statues'. Ask the children to dance until the music stops when they must sit down quickly or freeze like a statue.
8. Introduce 'Musical mats' which is the same as musical chairs, but with carpet tiles that are easier to remove!

Whatever next

- Ask the children to share ideas for any other group games using music or movement that they have played before at home, nursery, parties, etc.
- Try making up some new music games with the children.

All rounders

PSED: These games will provide lots of opportunities for children to work together, play co-operatively, take turns, and take account of one another's ideas.
CL: Ask the children to give instructions to another group on how to play a particular game. How will they start? What do the players need to know? Could they write down the instructions with your help?
UW: Try some games from around the world such as 'Escargot' - a French version of Hopscotch with a chalk pattern that looks like a snail full of numbers.

Supporting children with EAL in the early years

Chapter Nine: Movement and dance

Dance to your daddy

Try some simple dance moves and activities to help children with EAL to relax and enjoy moving to music.

What you need:

- A selection of music to dance to
- Some musical instruments
- Song words or version of the song online at www.bbc.co.uk/learning/schoolradio/subjects/earlylearning/nurserysongs
- Scarves, ribbons, hoops
- Parachute

What to do:

1. Sit all the children in a circle or on the carpet. Learn some finger rhymes and songs about dancing such as 'Dance to your daddy', 'Dance, Thumbkin, dance' or 'Little Johnny dances, on my thumb he dances'.
2. Teach the songs by singing each line for children to repeat or watch a version online.
3. Try some simple warm up activities. Ask children to sit with their toes pointing in to the middle of the circle. Can they flex their feet and make their toes wave to everybody? Ask them to sit up tall, stretch forward and touch their toes.
4. Stand up in the circle and to the count of 4, walk on the spot, stamp 4 times, stand on tip toe, and hop up and down. Try singing and moving to the 'Hokey Cokey'.
5. Talk about dancing and invite children to share their dance moves together by playing some of the music games from 'Somebody says', page 61. Encourage children with EAL to share any dances they know from home.
6. Play some music with a strong beat and invite children to clap along to the music and then to dance. Use music children have been listening to in the 'Listening corner', page 23 or 'Sounds of home', page 24.
7. Try some simple circle dance moves. Stand in a circle and walk on the spot in time to the beat. Count 1-8 in time to the beat, so children can learn to feel the phrases in the music. Take two steps forwards, two steps backwards. Turn around and walk on the spot again.
8. Use some small equipment such as scarves, ribbons on sticks or hoops.
9. Ask children to work with a partner. Invite them to face their partner and try some simple clapping patterns in time to the beat. Try holding hands and spinning their partner round.

Whatever next

- Try some parachute activities with the group. These are great for developing coordination and can be accompanied by movement, music and songs.
- Find out if any staff or family members are dancers and would like to try some more formal group choreography with the children.

All rounders

PSED: Encourage children with EAL to work together as part of a larger group and to follow instructions by watching each other. Invite more confident children to show off their dance skills to the group by setting up a 'dance hotspot' in the classroom.
UW: Watch some dances from around the world on YouTube. If any children at your setting know different dances from their home countries invite them to share.

Chapter Nine: Movement and dance

Yoga for kids

Share some simple and creative yoga positions with the children and salute the sun together.

What you need:

- Space and time for yoga
- Mats
- Online access for support and more ideas
- Music
- Pens, paper and paints

What to do:

1. Start with some research. Visit websites such as www.cosmickids.com or www.kidsyogastories.com and practise some yoga poses yourself.
2. Ask the children to find a space or a mat to sit on. Make sure that they can stretch out their hands wide and still not touch anybody.
3. Explain to children with EAL that you are going to do some yoga practice together. Remind them to try each movement carefully and not to rush. Just try for 10-15 minutes to start with as it's hard to concentrate for much longer.
4. Warm up with a sun salutation. Stand up tall with the feet together and pointing forward. Hands start by the side. Breathe in and lift the arms up high into the sky (mountain pose). Breathe out and lower the arms down to the ground like a ragdoll. Let the head and arms feel heavy.
5. Try some animal poses. Start with 'downward facing dog'. Stand with feet, hip width apart, on the floor. Place hands on the ground and push bottom in the air! Can they walk along on hands and feet and turn this into a 'bear' pose?
6. The frog pose is a familiar one - a squatting position with feet apart, knees out and hands on the floor. Turn it into a butterfly by sitting on the floor, straight back, hands holding feet together.
7. Try a plank pose, feet on the floor, heels raised, hands on the floor, and back straight - the crocodile. Place body down onto the floor, peel chest off the floor and look up as it turns into a snake - the cobra.
8. Finish the yoga practice with a cool down exercise. Try rest or child position - kneel down and sit back onto the feet, stretch arms out and breathe deeply. Wait until the heart rate returns to normal.

Whatever next

- Use stories to introduce the different poses and to create links between them. The children will enjoy using the stories to accompany the poses.
- Invite children to draw or paint some pictures of the animals involved in the yoga poses.
- Take photos of the children holding different poses and display alongside their artwork for parents/carers and visitors to see.

All rounders

PSED: Invite a yoga teacher to come and run a class for parents/carers and children at your setting as an introduction to yoga and fund raiser. Ask children to make posters advertising the event.
CL: Read some animal stories to the children, such as 'Just so Stories' by Rudyard Kipling. Encourage children to make up and act out some stories involving different animals from the yoga workout.
PD: Lots of the yoga moves and stretches will develop control and co-ordination skills.

Chapter Ten: Drama and expressive play

These activities allow children to use drama skills, character work, role play, miming games, partner ideas, improvised drama scenarios and puppets to express themselves in different ways. Drama games are a great starting point for any group activity and can be used to introduce new topics in a creative way. Mime is, of course, an essential part of communicating in the early stages of language development. Don't be afraid to go 'in role' and join in a drama game to increase the learning potential.

How to help children with EAL: Lots of drama activities involve small groups working together. This provides children with EAL with lots of opportunities to learn closely from their peers.

You can:
- use mime games to start activities in early stages
- provide lots of props and dressing up clothes for role-play activities
- try some group drama activities and share with parents.

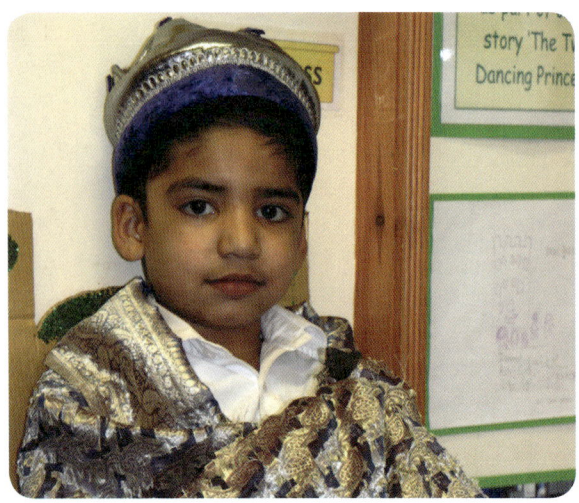

Chapter Ten: Drama and expressive play

The feeling hat

Children with EAL can use drama activities to get in touch with their feelings and express themselves more confidently.

What you need:

- A large floppy hat
- Lots of different hats
- Props
- Dressing up clothes
- Emojis
- Paper plates
- Felt pens
- Wooden spoons
- Blackboard paint
- Chalks

What to do:

1. Start by singing 'If you're happy and you know it' or 'Smile, smile, smile with me' and then change the emotions, see 'If you're happy and you know it', on page 20.
2. Warm up their faces by massaging each part with two fingers - cheeks, forehead, chin, jaw, eyebrows, and so on.
3. Play 'Pass a smile' around the circle. Start by turning to the child next to you and giving them a great big smile. Invite them to pass it round the ring. Repeat with different feelings.
4. Introduce the 'Feeling Hat'. Let children take turns to wear the hat. Explain that when they are wearing the hat their face must choose an expression or feeling. Can the other children guess what they are feeling?
5. Use feeling plates or emojis for children with EAL to suggest different feelings. Alternatively, use a set of the drama spoons (see All rounders). The child wearing the 'Feeling Hat' has to copy this feeling.
6. Extend the feeling to body language. Ask children to show how their bodies will look when they are happy, sad, angry, tired, bored, scared, etc.
7. Let children use dressing up clothes and props to extend their character work. They can dress up as characters from rhymes or stories or make up their own characters. Encourage children to go into role and use suitable language.
8. Ask for volunteers to show their dramatic characterisations to the group. Film them using a tablet.

Whatever next

- Make a set of drama spoons. Paint the dish part of some wooden spoons with blackboard paint. Leave to dry and draw some simple faces on them in chalk showing different feelings. Let children use these in the hat games. Whichever spoon is pulled out shows how they must feel.
- Play 'Pass me my hat'. Sit in a circle with a selection of different hats in the middle. Children take turns to choose a hat and assume the character the hat suggests. They can mime or use a line to show their character. Use the drama spoons to add a feeling.

All rounders

L: Make a list of feeling words. Ask children to make some cards with feeling words written on to use alongside the paper plates or drama spoons. Provide a set of photos of children showing different feelings. Can children match words to the pictures?
CL: The drama spoons can also be used to create stories. Rub off the feeling faces and let children draw new objects, words or characters to use in an original story or drama. The spoons can be used like puppets if it helps EAL children to feel more confident.

Supporting children with EAL in the early years

Chapter Ten: Drama and expressive play

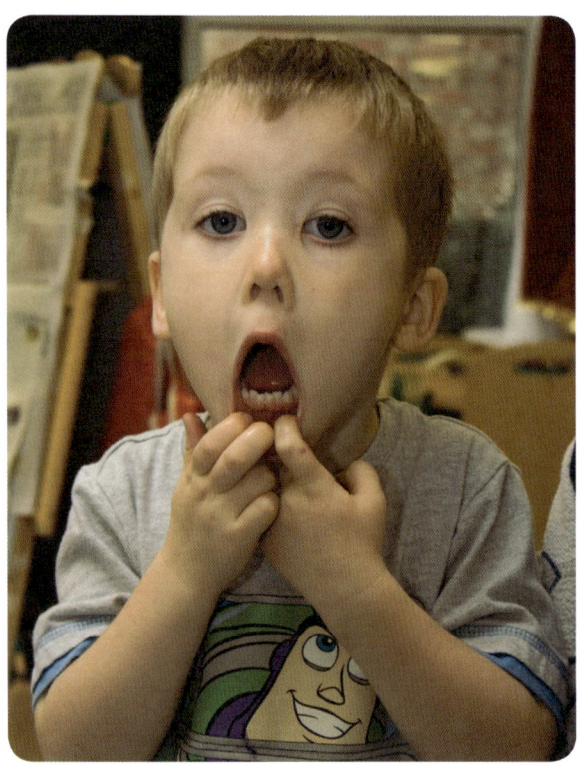

Mime time

These mime games are a great way for all the children to join in drama activities without worrying about words.

What you need:

- Space and time for some mimes
- Character cards - a sad child, an angry teacher, a bored parent, somebody who has fallen over, a thief, somebody scoring a goal, and so on
- Props - key, newspaper, jewellery, book, toy, egg cup, feather, saucepan, comb, toothbrush, frisbee, etc.

What to do:

1. Start by explaining mime as drama without words. This makes it an excellent introduction to drama activities for EAL children who are nervous of speaking to a group.
2. Warm up with some facial stretches - alternate between big smiley pumpkin faces and tiny screwed up prunes. Then stretch out all the other parts of the body so they are flexible and ready to express more than words.
3. Play 'Follow your finger'. Ask children to find a space on their own in the room. Ask them to move about, taking care not to bump into anybody else until you say 'stop'. Can they move again this time stretching out their little finger and pretending to follow it wherever it goes. Repeat with different parts of the body: nose, toe, elbow, knee, and so on.
4. Try some partner games. Play 'Mirrors' (see 'This is me' on page 46). Try 'The Sculptor'. Ask children to pretend to be a sculptor and the clay. The sculptor has to pretend to model the clay into a statue, moving limbs, head, body into a pleasing position. Remind them not to talk! Then swap over.
5. Ask the children to sit in a circle and play some group games. Start with 'In the magic box'. Pretend to place a magic box in the middle of the circle. Mime opening the box and take out what's inside. Can the children guess what it is by watching your mime? Let them take turns at miming what is 'in the magic box'.
6. Try a group game of 'What's my line?'. Either let children choose a job or action to mime or give them character cards. Take it in turns to come into the middle of the circle and mime an activity or character for the other children to guess.
7. Use mime to tell all or part of a story either from a picture book or a traditional tale.

Whatever next

- Try some improvised drama using props. Sit in a circle and choose a prop from a collection and mime using it correctly. Let children take turns to do the same.
- Play 'Whatever is it now?'. Show children how to mime using a prop so that it becomes something else, for instance - a feather could be used as a paintbrush, to clean teeth, as a pen, a conductor's baton, a tennis bat, a hairbrush, a spoon, and so on. Explain to children with EAL that you are 'pretending'.
- Film the children's dramas and mimes so they can watch themselves.

All rounders

CL: Let children make up their own stories to present to the group in mime.
L: Ask children to make up and write their own character cards for some mime activities.
PD: Encourage children to use bold movements and gestures in their mimes.

Chapter Ten: Drama and expressive play

Puppet power

Let children use puppets to make friends, invent stories, and try out some drama games.

What you need:

- Space and time for some drama
- Puppet
- Lots of different puppets - finger, hand, string, pop-up, etc.
- Paper and pens
- Fabric, felt, scissors
- Yoghurt or cream pots
- Sticks

What to do:

1. Introduce a special puppet to the children. They may be familiar with a particular puppet if you use one in your teaching regularly, see 'Echo Singing', on page 12 and 'Now I know my ABC', on page 18.
2. If you haven't used a puppet before, now is the time to make introductions, pick a name, and write a back story. Let children spend time making friends with the puppet through circle games and drama activities.
3. Warm up with an activity that uses their hands as animals without a puppet. Turn the finger and thumbs into a moving beak of a bird. Let one hand become a spider crawling up the other arm. Encourage the children to make these hand characters.
4. Talk about types of puppets and show the children how the different kinds of puppets work.
5. Sit in a circle and pass the different puppets round so children have an opportunity to handle them and use them to talk to each other.
6. Let children with EAL work with a talk partner and choose a puppet to use together.
7. Encourage children to make their puppets speak. They can use their own voice or make up a voice for the puppet. Record the children using the puppets together.
8. Set up a puppet theatre and let children work with a partner to create a show or story for an audience.
9. Encourage children to act out a well-known traditional story, a picture book, or make up a story, using themselves and the puppets.

Whatever next

- Try making your own puppets. Use a piece of paper to make a folded puppet, see 'Paper Crafts', on page 59.
- Make sock puppets. Ask children to bring in an old sock from home, the more colourful the better. Stick or sew buttons for eyes, add felt ears and show children how to put their hand into the sock and operate the puppet.
- Ask children to work with a partner and make up some stories using their sock puppets.

All rounders

PD: Play the 'Puppet master'. Explain to the children that they are all going to pretend to be puppets and move only when you tell them. Use a string puppet or marionette at the front of the room, so children can see which limb is being moved and try to copy. Remind them to move very stiffly as if they are made of wood like Pinocchio.

M: Use finger puppets to practise some simple number rhymes such as 'Five little speckled frogs' or 'Five little ducks'. Make some paper or felt frog or duck finger puppets to act out the rhyme.

Supporting children with EAL in the early years

Resources

References

Primary National Strategy 2007
Supporting children learning English as an additional language
Guidance for practitioners in the EYFS, Department for children, schools and families

Collaboration between 3- and 4-Year-Olds in Self-Initiated Play on Instruments
Susan Young, International Journal of Educational Research, 2008, Vol.47(1), p.3-10

Active Learning through Formative Assessment
Shirley Clarke, (Hodder Education) 2008

Development Matters in the Early Years Foundation Stage (EYFS) 2012, Early Education

Websites

www.pocketcultures.com

www.bbc.co.uk/learning/schoolradio/subjects/earlylearning/nurserysongs

www.mamalisa.com

www.learnenglishkids.britishcouncil.org

www.worldmusic.net

www.womad.co.uk

www.amazingmorph.com

www.origami-instructions.com/origami-for-kids.html

www.cosmickids.com

www.kidsyogastories.com

Children's books

Little Beaver and the Echo by Amy MacDonald (Puffin Books) 1998

The Leopard's Drum by Jessica Souhami (Frances Lincoln) 2006

Rocks could Sing: A Discovered Alphabet by Lesley McGuirk (Tricycle Press) 2011

I Love You, Blue Kangaroo by Emma Chichester Clark (Andersen Press) 2015

Big Yellow Digger by Julia Jarman (Orchard Books) 2012

Stick Man by Julia Donaldson (Alison Green Books) 2016

Robot Rumpus by Sean Taylor (Andersen Press) 2014

Funny Bones by Allan Ahlberg (Puffin) 1999